A Vast and Magnificent Land

1 "Deux Rivières Portage, On the Red River
Route," from a sketch by William
Armstrong, published in the Canadian
Illustrated News, October 14, 1871.

PLATE 2

A Vast and

Magnificent Land

An Illustrated History of Northern Ontario

EDITED BY MATT BRAY AND ERNIE EPP

 LAKEHEAD UNIVERSITY

LAURENTIAN UNIVERSITY

A Bicentennial Project of the
ONTARIO MINISTRY OF NORTHERN AFFAIRS

PLATE 3

Lakehead University ISBN 0-88663-001-0
Laurentian University ISBN 0-88667-002-0

Canadian Cataloguing in Publication Data

Main entry under title:
A Vast and magnificent land

"A bicentennial project of the Ontario Ministry of Northern Affairs."
Bibliography: p.
ISBN 0-88663-001-0 (Lakehead University).—
ISBN 0-88667-002-0 (Laurentian University)

1. Ontario – History. I. Bray, Robert Matthew. II. Epp, A. Ernest, 1941–

FC3094.4.V37 1984   971.3'1   C84-099125-8
F1057.V37 1984

Published by Lakehead University, Thunder Bay, Ontario P7B 5E1 and Laurentian University, Sudbury, Ontario P3E 2C6. Made possible by generous assistance from the Ontario Ministry of Northern Affairs.

CO-ORDINATING EDITOR: John Eerkes
PRODUCTION CO-ORDINATOR: Sandra Sims
PHOTO EDITOR: Mac Swackhammer
PHOTO RESEARCHERS:
  SUDBURY: Gwenda Hallsworth
                Kathleen M. Brankley
                Brian Hart
  THUNDER BAY: Elinor Barr
                Peter Elliott
  TORONTO: Mac Swackhammer
DESIGN: Brant Cowie/Artplus Ltd.
TYPESETTING: Imprint Typesetting
PRINTING: Bradbury Tamblyn & Boorne Ltd.
BINDING: The Bryant Press Ltd.

CELEBRATING TOGETHER · FÊTONS ÇA ENSEMBLE
1784 · ONTARIO · 1984 ·

A Bicentennial Project of the
ONTARIO MINISTRY OF
NORTHERN AFFAIRS
1984
Hon. Leo Bernier, Minister
David Hobbs, Deputy Minister

Contents

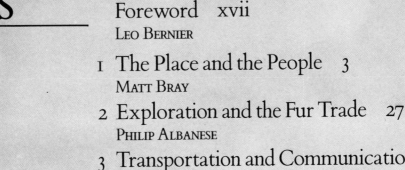

2 William Armstrong's watercolour paintings
3 of life along the north shore of Lake Superior
were greatly admired during his lifetime.
Born in Dublin in 1822, he was sent to
England in 1838 to apprentice as a railway
construction engineer. He came to Canada in
1851, settled in Toronto, and later worked on
the construction of the CPR rail line through
Northern Ontario. His art provides a
valuable record of the region in the late 19th
century. He died in 1914. 2, Magpie Falls at

Michipicoten, painted by Armstrong in
1901. 3, an undated watercolour by
Armstrong depicting an Indian encampment
on White Fish Island in the late 19th
century.

4 Soon after Manitoulin Island became an
5 Indian reserve in 1838, French Jesuit
6 missionaries arrived to minister to the
inhabitants. In August 1847 Father
Auguste Kohler joined the Ste. Croix

mission just in time to witness the annual
Indian gathering at Manitowaning, where
the government distributed "presents" such
as arms, blankets, and knives. These three
paintings of the Manitowaning meeting were
made by Father Kohler and now reside in
France. 4, the annual gathering for the
distribution of government presents at
Manitowaning village. About 2,000 Indians
attended the 1847 meeting. 5, the large log
chapel at Manitowaning was part of the

Roman Catholic mission. On the right, a flag marks the Methodist chief's wigwam. 6, Father Kohler said his first mass among the Ojibwa on August 7, 1847 in the log house on the left. The cross was tall and made of white metal so that it would be visible across the bay.

7. William Armstrong accompanied the Wolseley Red River expedition in 1870-71 as chief engineer, with the rank of captain. This watercolour, painted in 1901, shows the expedition encamped, perhaps at Sault Ste. Marie.

8. "Rat Portage, Lake of the Woods, Keewatin," from a photograph by J.K. Salter, published in the Canadian Illustrated News, October 9, 1880. At that time Canada and Ontario both claimed jurisdiction over the area.

7

8

9 *Pointe de Meuron, pictured here about 1882, is today the site of the reconstruction of Old Fort William.*

10 *The first Anglican mission in Sault Ste. Marie was established in 1832. St. Luke's Anglican Church was built in 1870 to serve the growing congregation. This picture of the church was painted in 1945.*

11 *Little Current Village, or "Webidjiwang," Manitoulin Island, around 1873. Drawing by Michael Metosage.*

POINTE DE MEURON.

10

11

12 "The 7th Battalion (Fusiliers) of London, Entertained at Port Arthur," based on a photograph and published in the Illustrated War News of Toronto on May 9, 1885.

13 "Arrival of the Royal Grenadiers at Camp Desolation," from a sketch by Color Sergeant F. W. Curzon, published in the Illustrated War News, April 18, 1885.

The railway in the background transported the Canadian Expeditionary Force to deal with the Riel Rebellion of 1885.

14 Sailing at Desbarats, in the North Channel of Lake Huron.

15 Until the arrival of the bush planes in the late 1920s, dog teams were used to travel to otherwise inaccessible areas. This team worked in the Temagami area, around 1910.

16 Lumbermen going to the woods, Sturgeon River, around the turn of the century.

17 *In 1908 Cobalt was a boom town. Tents housed recent arrivals who couldn't be accommodated at the Prospect Hotel (centre).*

18 *Birch Street in Chapleau, about 1910. The CPR opened up the district's forest and mineral wealth in 1885.*

19 *North Bay early established itself as a transportation and supply centre for the lumbering, farming, and mining industries. This is Main Street in 1910.*

20 *The timber trestle at the Algoma Central Railway's mile 104 in the Agawa Valley, 1916.*

21

Foreword

THIS YEAR ONTARIO celebrates its Bicentennial, marking 200 years of progress and growth.

The boundaries of Northern Ontario as we know it are less than 100 years old, but this story begins much earlier. In 1670 the expanse of territory in our northwest drained by rivers emptying into Hudson Bay was administered by the Hudson's Bay Company. When the company transferred these lands to the Dominion after Confederation, the new provinces pressed their claims to the territory.

Ontario's claim to the land as far west as the Lake of the Woods, north to the Albany River, and east to Quebec was upheld in a Privy Council decision in 1884 and proclaimed in the 1889 Canada (Ontario Boundary) Act. However, not until 1912 was that part of the District of Keewatin which defines our northernmost provincial land added to Ontario.

During the past 200 years Northern Ontario has seen a remarkable development of its resources, industries, communities, and people. Along the way it has made a significant contribution to this province's overall history and development. What was seen by a handful of European adventurers as a vast and sparsely populated wilderness has become what we know Northern Ontario to be today—a resource-rich land supporting modern urban centres linked through a network of rails, roads, air routes, and electronic wizardry. This book is about the people and events that brought about this remarkable transition.

As Minister of Northern Affairs it gives me great pleasure to present this illustrated history of Northern Ontario as our ministry's contribution to the Bicentennial celebrations of the entire province.

To prepare this work, twelve authors were asked to write short summaries of major themes in the history of Northern Ontario. The authors were selective in what they chose to discuss, and each topic is dealt with succinctly. Yet each chapter in the book gives us a framework within which to view Northern Ontario's past and serves to place the historical photographs in context.

The photographs were gathered by three teams of researchers who collected more than 3,000 photographs from sources throughout the north and in major southern cities. Many northern residents supplied photos from their private collections. Only about 10 percent of the submitted photos could be chosen, and they were selected specifically to illustrate our ten themes.

We are grateful to the many northerners who responded to our requests for information and photographs. Institutions both large and small were most helpful. Everyone who lent time and energy to this project has helped to illustrate a vital and eventful past.

I commend our two contributing editors, Ernie Epp of Lakehead University in Thunder Bay and Matt Bray of Laurentian University in Sudbury, for being willing to attempt a difficult task and for guiding the text to its successful completion.

I am proud of our accomplishments in Northern Ontario. Through hard work and commitment we have contributed not only to our own well-being, but to that of many others throughout the province and the rest of Canada. I hope this book will stimulate continuing research into the history of Northern Ontario and serve as a lasting contribution to a better understanding of a still-growing north.

Leo Bernier
Minister of Northern Affairs

A Vast and Magnificent Land

CHAPTER ONE

The Place and the People

MATT BRAY
Associate Professor of History,
Laurentian University,
Sudbury.

1–1 *A May Day demonstration in Timmins in the 1920s. These miners and their families are protesting against piece-work speedups, which increased the number of accidents in the mines. Concern about occupational health and safety was one of the factors in the formation of the mine unions.*

1–2 *Native women and children with their pets at Flying Post, 1906. By this time the influx of settlers had reduced the proportion of Northern Ontario's native population to less than 10% of the total population.*

1–3 *The Abelard Clement family in Biscotasing, around 1908. The town was booming at the time; a lumber mill and a post office had just been built in the community, which had begun in 1880 as a CPR survey camp. When the mill closed in 1927, the number of jobs declined and many residents left the town.*

1–2

1–3

1–4 Northern Ontario's pioneers brought modern technology, fashions, and attitudes with them. Mrs. Archie Bishop and her family settled in Gillies Township near Hymers around 1903, when she had this portrait taken.

1–5 James Fletcher, an Ojibwa, served the White River, Missanabie, and Chapleau areas as an Anglican catechist (lay religious instructor) for 42 years. He died in 1944.

1–6 R.E. Redman, first chief ranger of Quetico Park, in 1910. Quetico was set aside as a forest reserve in 1909 to protect game, particularly moose, and was made a provincial park in 1913.

1–4

1–5

1–6

1-7 The Boy Scouts were first organized in Canada in 1908 and incorporated by an act of Parliament in 1914. The movement aimed to develop boys' character and skills to prepare them for adulthood. This Fort Frances group posed in front of the McIrvine School around 1920.

1-8 The first settlers in the gold-producing areas of Swastika, Chaput Hughes, and Kirkland Lake came to work the mining camps. About half of the population was British; the other half consisted of French, Finnish, Yugoslavian, Polish, and Ukrainian immigrants. The Swastika hockey team of 1911 reflected this ethnic mix. The names recorded for this team were John Gaudaur, Jack Furlong, Sid Antram, and Jack Lingenfelter.

1-7

1-8

A CENTURY AGO the place was called "New Ontario." Today it is simply "Northern Ontario." Whatever the name, since time began that part of the province to the north and west of a line drawn by the Mattawa River, Lake Nipissing, and the French River has possessed its own unique character. Throughout history it has cast its spell far and wide, conjuring up diverse and conflicting images in the minds of those it has so captivated.

In some it has stirred romantic visions of an untamed wilderness, inhabited by hardy adventurers living in harmony with nature—the original "True North, strong and free." For others it has evoked quite a different picture, one of a cold, isolated, forbidding land that continuously challenges the right of man even to exist within its confines.

Northern Ontario has been cursed as a great rocky barrier, splitting the upper half of the North American continent and hampering the orderly, westward movement of first the French, then the British, and finally Canadians themselves. It has also been blessed as a limitless storehouse of natural resources—furs, timber, minerals, and agricultural lands. As this brief review of its geography and history reveals, these images both mask and reflect the realities of life in Ontario's northland.

Most of Northern Ontario's 85 million hectares lie within the Canadian Shield, a rugged, hilly, lake-pocked plateau, ranging in height from 300 to 600 metres above sea level, which swirls around Hudson Bay in horseshoe fashion from Labrador in the east to the Arctic in the northwest. In geological terms the shield is defined by its ancient Precambrian bedrock, one to three billion years old, which contains the mineral wealth so vital to the Northern Ontario economy.

To the north is the Hudson Bay Lowland, a coastal plain 150 to 300 kilometres wide that slopes gradually to the Hudson and James bays. It differs from the shield in having a base of younger sedimentary rocks dating from the Paleozoic age, about 400 million years ago. Quite distinct from both the lowland and the shield is Manitoulin Island, whose limestone and shale formations are an extension of the Niagara Escarpment of Southern Ontario.

Differences in climate have created distinct vegetation zones. The more temperate southern sections of the Canadian Shield are covered with mixed forests of deciduous (leaf-shedding) trees such as birch, maple, and poplar, and conifers such as spruce, pine, fir, tamarack, and cedar. In the cooler north, conifers are most common. The Hudson Bay Lowland, plagued by poor drainage and waterlogged soils, has few protective trees.

In the shaping of the topography of the north, the most significant era was the Ice Age that occurred within the past fifty thousand years. During this period both the Hudson Bay Lowland and the Canadian Shield were blanketed by continental glaciers. As the glaciers advanced they wore down hills, gouged depressions, carved out stream and river beds, and scraped off the topsoil. Their retreat exposed a bare, rocky terrain dotted with many small lakes and a few immense ones. As the larger lakes receded, they left flat lakebeds that gave the north its limited agricultural potential. The best known of these are the Great Clay Belt in the Hearst-Cochrane area and its extension, the Little Clay Belt, north of Lake Timiskaming.

Geography, geology, and climate have been crucial in moulding the history of Northern Ontario. They have influenced what countries have claimed it, what peoples have inhabited it, where they have settled, and how they have lived.

The ancestors of the North American native peoples probably entered Northern Ontario about nine thousand years ago, settling along the shores of the upper Great Lakes not then covered by glaciers. Big-game-hunting Paleo Indians of the Plano Culture may have been the first to move into the area. They were followed by hunting, gathering, and fishing cultures: the Shield Culture of the Archaic period (7,000 to 3,000 years ago); the Laurel Culture, pottery-using people of the Initial Woodland period (3,000 to 1,000 years ago); and finally the Algonkian Culture of the Terminal Woodland period (1,000 to 250 years ago).

By the 17th century the native population had developed a seasonal woodland lifestyle centred on hunting and trading. They spoke the Algonkian language but were divided into a number of dialect groups, for example, the Ojibwa and the Cree. They were grouped into autonomous bands, small groups of hunters loosely connected by marriage and clan ties. Some of these bands, still clearly distinguishable today, were the Mississagis of the Mississagi River area, the Nipissing of Garden River, and the Dokis of Lake Nipissing. Other groups included the Sauteurs at Sault Ste. Marie; the Gens du Nord, Kilistinons, and Bagouache, north of Lake Superior and east of Lake Nipigon; the Alamepigons at Lake Nipigon; and the Outaouacs west of Lake Nipigon.

At the beginning of the 17th century, representatives of two European powers appeared on the fringes of Northern Ontario—England's Henry Hudson on Hudson Bay

and France's Samuel de Champlain in the Georgian Bay area. Neither France nor Great Britain pressed territorial claims to the area until 1670, when King Charles II of England granted a trading charter to the Hudson's Bay Company that encompassed the entire Hudson Bay drainage basin. The French responded in 1671 and 1672 by sending expeditions to proclaim the area as their own, and a rivalry that would last for nearly a century was on in earnest.

In the course of this commercial and imperial competition, neither country "occupied" Northern Ontario in the conventional sense. The French were *voyageurs*, land mariners criss-crossing a great wooded sea. Apart from causing the gradual depletion of the fur-bearing animals, they did not seriously disturb the environment. The British were even less obtrusive; until the French encroachment on their fur preserves became unbearable in the 1740s, they remained firmly anchored to the shores of Hudson Bay.

France's elimination from North America in 1763 placed all of Northern Ontario in the hands of Great Britain, either directly or via the Hudson's Bay Company, but otherwise little changed. The Indian fur traders who had been allies of New France transferred their allegiances to the Scottish-French partnerships that made up the Montreal-based North West Company, formed in the late 1770s. From then until their merger in 1821 it and the Hudson's Bay Company battled fiercely for commercial primacy in the north.

When the southern Great Lakes-to-Montreal fur-trading system was abandoned in 1821, Northern Ontario was briefly isolated. During this time the contacts of the small native, British, and French populations were with Great Britain via the Hudson's Bay Company, but these contacts were few and far between. In the 1820s and 1830s, even though the Province of Upper Canada was judicially responsible for the north, Canadian interest was limited mainly to the isolated missionary activities of the Roman Catholic, Anglican, and Methodist churches in the Lake Timiskaming-Moose River area, on Manitoulin

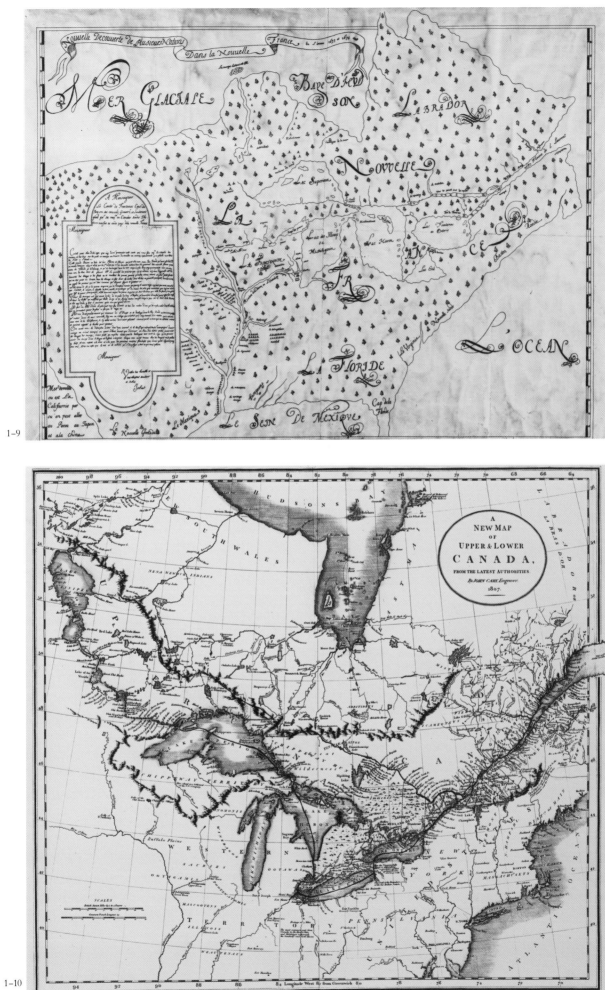

1–9

1–10

Island, at Michipicoten, and in the Thunder Bay and Rainy River districts.

In the mid-1840s Canadians became aware of the economic potential of the north. Lumbering leaped from the Ottawa Valley westward to Lake Timiskaming and Lake Nipissing, bringing with it a mixture of French and British peoples. Then the mineral resources were discovered, first at Bruce Mines and later at Michipicoten. These prospects prompted the Canadian government to send W. B. Robinson, provincial commissioner of Indian affairs, to negotiate with the Ojibwa for title to their land. The result was the signing of two treaties in 1850, one involving the lands west from Batchawana Bay to the Pigeon River and the other east from Batchawana Bay to Penetanguishene. This cleared the way for Canadians to settle the area immediately north of the upper Great Lakes.

A substantial Canadian presence in Northern Ontario became viable in the 1850s and 1860s. In 1855 the construction of a canal at Sault Ste. Marie by the Americans and the completion of the Northern Railway linking Toronto and Collingwood opened up Lake Superior, especially the Thunder Bay region, to regular contact with Southern Ontario. In the early 1860s Manitoulin Island, which had been an Indian reserve for thirty years, was thrown open to non-Indian use. This resulted in a flood of immigrants, mostly Protestants of British descent, who completely altered its ethnic character in the following twenty years.

The Confederation of the British North American colonies in 1867 had little impact on Northern Ontario. The union merely confirmed the Great Lakes watershed as part of the new Province of Ontario. More crucial was Canada's acquisition of Rupert's Land from the Hudson's Bay Company in 1870. After exactly two hundred years of political separation, the geographic Siamese twins of Northern Ontario to the north and south of the main height-of-land were finally joined together.

Northern Ontario was still not fully reunited politically. It was not clear whether the newly acquired lands were under the jurisdiction of the federal government or that of Ontario. Since both prestige and control over

incalculably valuable forest and mining resources were at stake, each side was determined to prevail. The battle began in 1872 between the federal Conservative administration of Sir John A. Macdonald and the provincial Liberal regime of Oliver Mowat. It was set in abeyance in the mid-1870s during the prime ministership of Alexander Mackenzie, like Mowat a Liberal, and then picked up again with Macdonald's return to power in 1878. From then until 1884 the situation in the disputed Lake of the Woods-Rainy River area became a comic opera, as both levels of government tried to enforce their own laws and regulations and ended up arresting each other's law agents. In 1883 the citizens of Rat Portage (now Kenora) voted in the provincial elections of both Manitoba and Ontario.

By 1884 it was obvious that the failure to settle the boundary question was hindering the development of Northwestern Ontario. The issue was submitted for arbitration to the highest court in the Empire, the Judicial Committee of the Privy Council in Great Britain. To Ontario's delight and the federal government's chagrin, the committee ruled in favour of the province. It established Ontario's western boundary at the northwest angle of the Lake of the Woods and its northern boundary at the Albany and English rivers. During the next four years Macdonald vainly attempted to have this decision modified, so that in 1889 the British parliament passed the Canada (Ontario Boundary) Act. This still left the area north of the Albany and English rivers outside of the province's control, a problem resolved in 1912, when the Borden administration transferred the Patricia district, until then part of Keewatin, to Ontario. Northern Ontario's boundaries were finally set.

By then Northern Ontario had acquired most of the human characteristics that distinguish it from the rest of the province. In 1871 its population was barely fifteen thousand people, 25 percent of whom lived either on Manitoulin Island or in the two central-Algoma towns of Bruce Mines and Sault Ste. Marie. The rest were scattered around Lake Timiskaming, Killarney, the Spanish

1-12 The initial contact between the native people and Europeans was usually made by a trader or a missionary; at times they travelled together. Father Evan was the Oblate priest at Bear Island, Lake Temagami, at the turn of the century. The Oblate Missionaries of Mary Immaculate was a Roman Catholic order responsible for missions in remote areas. Founded in France, it entered Canada in 1841 and conducted missionary work in the Ottawa River and Hudson Bay districts.

1-13 Although Manitoulin Island had been set aside as an Indian reserve in 1836, its timber and agricultural potential soon attracted white settlers. Mai-she-quong-gai was one of the Ojibwa chiefs who signed a treaty in 1862 that transferred most of Manitoulin Island to the Crown. Non-Indian settlement of the island began in the following year.

1-14 James Christie, the Hudson's Bay Co. factor at New Brunswick House, 1903. Until Canada acquired Rupert's Land in 1870, men like Christie administered the law and the economy in the fur-trade areas of Northern Ontario.

1-11

1-12

1-13

1-14

River, Batchewana, Michipicoten, Fort William, and St. Ignace Island.

The next forty years brought a considerable increase in population. The 1911 census registered 215,000 persons, and this population was much more dispersed across the north than it had been in 1871. This was so because by 1911 the factors responsible for determining the locations of communities and towns—resources and physical accessibility—had in most cases already been joined. The Canadian Pacific Railway, built in the early 1880s, had opened up new lumbering, mining, and agricultural areas, giving fresh life to already established towns such as Fort William and Rat Portage and bringing into existence many other communities, including North Bay, Sudbury, and Dryden. This process was repeated in the early 20th century with the construction of the Temiskaming and Northern Ontario, the Canadian Northern, and the National Transcontinental railways.

From the 1890s onward, provincial government policy greatly influenced the development of the north. While some regulations had already been passed concerning forestry and mining, only then did politicians come to see Northern Ontario as a place for long-term development and large-scale, permanent settlement. One man with this vision was John Dryden, a northern enthusiast who as minister of agriculture in the early 1890s was convinced that the area possessed an almost unlimited agricultural potential. His policies resulted in the colonization of the Wabigoon district, which now bears his name. The turn-of-the-century Liberal ministries of premiers Hardy and Ross shared this optimism; they adopted the "manufacturing condition" policies concerning logs and pulp and paper, and initiated the Temiskaming and Northern Ontario Railway project.

The first really successful northern politician was Frank Cochrane of Sudbury, who served as the provincial minister of lands, forests and mines from 1905 to 1911, a period in which the Ontario Provincial Police was formed to bring law and order to the frontier mining communities of the Porcupine. In 1911 Cochrane switched to the federal arena, where he became the Conservative minister of railways in the Borden administration. The new provincial minister of lands, forests and mines was W. H. Hearst of Sault Ste. Marie, who in 1914 became premier of Ontario, the only northerner ever to hold the office.

Just as railways, resources, and government policies combined to promote the development of the north, so they attracted a culturally diverse population. Here again by 1911 a pattern that has persisted to the modern era had become clear. In 1871 the population had been composed almost entirely of Canada's "founding peoples," Indians (50.3 percent), British (32.4 percent), and French (15.8 percent). By 1911 the figures were Indians 5.3, British 50.7, and French 21.2, while 23 percent came from other countries. Of these other ethnic groups, though the 1911 census did not use them as official designations, the two most prominent were Finns and Ukrainians, while there were slightly fewer Italians, Germans, and Scandinavians, and even smaller percentages of Poles, Dutch, Belgians, Swiss, Greeks, Chinese, and Japanese.

Perhaps because of deliberate choice, or perhaps simply because of historical accident, ethnic groups gravitated to particular communities and to particular types of work. The exceptions proving the rule were Canadians of British origin, who were to be found in significantly large numbers in all walks of life and in all parts of the north. French Canadians, who had gradually moved westward from Quebec, were located mainly in the lumbering, mining, and agricultural communities around Cobalt, North Bay, Sturgeon Falls, and Sudbury, bringing to Northeastern Ontario the vital duality characteristic of Canada at large.

Immigrants from continental Europe were urban-oriented and concentrated in a few selected areas. By far the largest number of Ukrainians lived in Fort William, but there were also sizable groups in Kenora, Copper Cliff, Sault Ste. Marie, North Bay, and Timmins. So too, Fort William was the Northern Ontario home of the largest single concentration of Finns, although here again smaller but still significant numbers lived in Port Arthur, Nipigon, Sault Ste. Marie, Copper Cliff, Cobalt, and

1–15

1–16

Timmins. In being more likely to take up agriculture in the districts surrounding these towns, Finns differed from other immigrants to the north. Italians were limited primarily to Fort William and Port Arthur in Northwestern Ontario, and Sault Ste. Marie, Copper Cliff, and North Bay in the northeast. Small Polish groups existed at Port Arthur-Fort William, Sault Ste. Marie, and Copper Cliff; and even smaller Scandinavian contingents were to be found in the Kenora-Rainy River-Fort Frances district, as well as at Fort William and Port Arthur.

Since 1911 both the economy and the population of Northern Ontario have grown in an irregular fashion. During the decade of the Great War the overall population of the north increased by 24 percent. Growth was especially strong in larger centres, partly as a result of the economic demands of the war, but also because of the policies of the Whitney and Hearst governments, which between 1912 and 1917 spent $10 million on road construction and improvements under the Northern Development Act of 1912.

In the 1920s Northern Ontario enjoyed, in terms of percentage, the largest population increase of the modern era—39 percent. Much of it was due to European immigration, and the ethnic diversity of the north was greatly enhanced. After 1923 the north was fortunate in having as premier at Queen's Park another northern enthusiast, the former minister of lands, forests and mines, G. Howard Ferguson, whose government actively promoted the area.

Though the total population of the north increased by 23 percent during the 1930s, this growth occurred mostly later in the decade and was unevenly distributed. The entire area was in economic doldrums until 1933, when the situation began to improve, especially in the mining communities of Timmins and Sudbury. This was one period when international economic realities overrode provincial government policies. At the beginning of the decade the Henry administration established the Ministry of Northern Development to make the north attractive to settlement and colonization, but in spite of spending nearly $15 million on projects such as the completion of the

Temiskaming and Northern Ontario Railway to Moosonee, it largely failed to meet its objectives.

On the other hand, the policy of the Hepburn Liberals who came into power in 1934 was quite the reverse. They abolished the Ministry of Northern Development, cut expenditures on such activities as forest fire regulation and control, abandoned the "manufacturing condition" on pulp and paper, and ended all assistance to colonization. Yet due to mining development Northern Ontario slowly recovered during their years in office.

During the 1940s Northern Ontario's population rose by only 17.5 percent, the smallest increase up to that point. Because they possessed resources or industries vital to the war effort, the communities that expanded in the early 1940s were Fort William and Port Arthur in the northwest and Sault Ste. Marie and Sudbury in the northeast. After the war, provincial government policies once again came into play. In 1945 the Drew government established the Provincial Institute of Mining at Haileybury, and in 1947 it fully restored the manufacturing condition on pulp and paper, causing production to triple in only two years.

In absolute numbers the single largest population increase in the history of Northern Ontario occurred in the 1950s, when it grew from 536,000 in 1951 to 722,000 in 1961. All sectors of the local economy boomed, though the leading industry was mining, which employed 20 percent of the workforce by the end of the decade. Like the 1920s, the 1950s were characterized by large-scale immigration from continental Europe, and Ontario's north, because of its well-established ethnic populations, again proved to be an attractive place for many such newcomers.

Its cultural diversity was strengthened in these years as the numbers of Ukrainians, Finns, Poles, Italians, Scandinavians, Czechs, Slovaks, Germans, Dutch, and others swelled to about 30 percent of the total population. The remaining population was 42 percent British and 28 percent French, making Northern Ontario a replica-in-miniature of the Canadian mosaic and distinguishing it markedly from the rest of the province.

The 1960s and 1970s presented a sharp contrast to the preceding decade. The population of Northern Ontario

1-19 Many prospectors spent their lives searching for ore and staking property without much luck. Johnny Jones searched for gold in the Timmins area during the 1909 rush and in the Red Lake area during the 1926 rush, both times without making a big strike.

1-20 James Wilmington Cross, born in Halton County in 1844, came to the Silver Islet Mine as a builder in 1870. He worked as a captain while in charge of an underground crew. When the mine closed in 1884, Captain Cross stayed on as caretaker and tended nearby navigation lights on Thunder Cape. He died in 1930.

1-21 Frances O'Connell, the first secretary of the Big Fork and Aylsworth Women's Institute. The Women's Institutes were founded in Southern Ontario in 1897 to allow women an opportunity to discuss their problems and to work together to improve the standards of homemaking, health, sanitation, and child rearing. The organization grew rapidly in the early 20th century as WIs sprang up across Canada.

1-17

1-18

1-19

1-20

1-21

rose by only 7 percent from 1961 to 1971, and not at all in the next ten years. Most of the growth in the 1960s resulted from the expansion of the nickel industry, but in the 1970s it too had its setbacks. Slowdowns also occurred in the other key sectors of the Northern Ontario economy—lumbering, pulp and paper, and tourism. Only in the early 1980s has expansion begun once again.

Today Northern Ontario is a fully defined place populated by men and women of diverse ethnic origins who are genuine northerners, either by birth or adoption. The transitional phases of unsettled migrants shifting from one area to the other or leaving altogether have ended. Northerners are now born, raised, and educated from kindergarten to community college or university graduation in both of Canada's official languages. They enter a workforce that has become infinitely more varied and complex, and they enjoy theatre, the arts, and other cultural activities as well as a wide range of outdoor recreational opportunities, all without ever leaving the north.

No longer is Northern Ontario simply a place in which to work or survive; rather it is a place in which three-quarters of a million Ontarians choose to live satisfying and productive lives. Ontario's north has finally come of age.

1-22

1-23 *The first graduating class of nurses at St. Joseph's Hospital in Sudbury, 1913. The Grey Nuns of the Cross had been in charge of the hospital since 1896.*

1-24 *Université de Sudbury, now federated with Laurentian University, began as Le Collège du Sacré-Coeur, a residential boys' school, established by the Jesuit order in 1913. It was the only French-language classical college in the province, outside of Ottawa. This photograph shows the staff and student body in 1916.*

1-23

1-24

1-25 *A World War I postcard from Cobalt.*

1-26 *Many Indian men served in the Great War. In 1917 John (Jimmy) Osheckemick enlisted at Chapleau for overseas service in the 227th Algoma Battalion. This portrait with his parents at Biscotasing was taken before he left for the front. After the war Osheckemick returned home to join the Canadian Forestry Corps; he died in 1961.*

1-27 *During the war thousands of women waited for their husbands and fathers to return. A photograph of a man in uniform sits on top of the piano in the home of Captain and Mrs. A.R. Johnston, Sault Ste. Marie.*

1-25

1-26

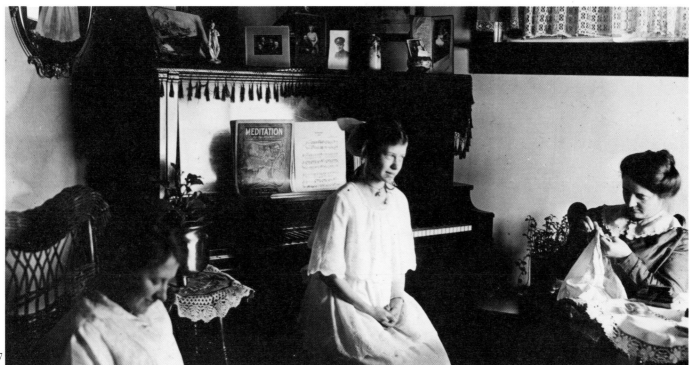

1-27

1-28 *A mother and her children stand by a fresh grave in Nipigon, around 1910. In 1914 the life expectancy for men was 46 years; for women, 49 years. The single most common cause of death was tuberculosis, but occupational accidents were also a major factor in the death rate.*

1-29 *Ukrainian workers at the Coniston smelter, around 1920. The clothing they wore offered virtually no protection against an accident in the smelter.*

1-28

1-29

1-30 *Freddy Beresford was a market gardener who provided vegetables to the townsfolk in the Ignace area in the 1920s. Here he displays some of the produce from his garden on the shores of Agimak Lake, near Moose Bay.*

1-31 *Until the 1940s wood was the main home-heating fuel in Northern Ontario. Chopping enough wood to heat even one home over the winter involved a substantial amount of work. Here school teacher Margaret Kennedy, left, and Mrs. Eugene Grenier split logs together in Chapleau in the 1920s.*

1-30

1-31

1-32 *Bishop David Joseph Scollard, Roman Catholic Bishop of Sault Ste. Marie from 1905 to 1934, travelled widely throughout Northern Ontario. In this photograph, taken in 1930, he presides over an open-air confirmation service.*

1-33 *Princess Maggie, seen here in 1927 with her friend Billie Leclair, was an Ojibwa trapper in the Timmins area.*

1-34 *The telephone switchboard was the nerve centre of a town's communication system. Sometimes the switchboard was located in the home of the woman who operated it. Annie Murchison, here pictured about 1923, was the first operator in Devlin.*

1-32

1-33

1-34

21

1-35 *With Northern Ontario's population spread along the railway lines, it was easier for health and education services to go to the people than for the people to come to them. These public health nurses travelled on a gasoline-powered railway car.*

1-36 *Unfortunately, bigotry has also played its part in the development of the north. The intermingling of cultures has produced a unique mosaic in Northern Ontario, but not without some conflict. These Timmins Jews were attacked by antisemites, probably in the 1940s; here they display the stick and stones thrown at them.*

1-35

1-36

1-37 Northern Ontario hosted a number of
1-38 prisoner-of-war camps during World War II.
Most of the inmates were Germans. In 1-37
guards and prisoners clown (?) at the Red
Rock POW camp around 1945. 1-38 is one
of the many illustrations from a sketchbook-
diary kept by a German POW in an
Espanola camp. The artist, "Charley,"
recorded his capture, his dreams (often those
of a love-starved man), and humorous
insights into camp life in his sketchbook.
Some prisoners chose to return to Northern
Ontario after the war.

1-39 During World War II about 22,000 people
of Japanese descent were transported from
British Columbia because they were thought
to pose a threat to national security. They
were "resettled" in internment camps from
the British Columbia interior to Ontario.
This Japanese internment camp was located
at Angler, near Marathon. Angler no longer
exists.

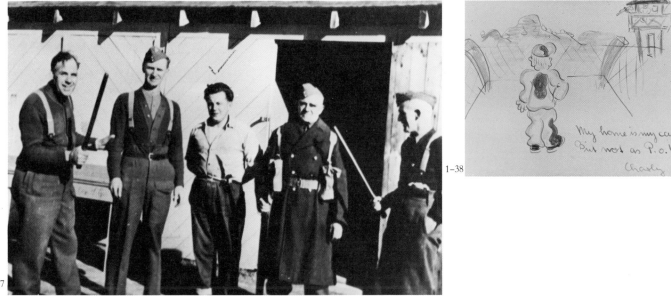

1-37

1-38

1-39

1-40 *During World War II women were mobilized to work in essential services, agriculture, and war industries. These women worked in surface operations at International Nickel to fill the void left by enlisted men.*

1-41 *Mrs. Lalonde with her husband and son, setting up a timber-salvage operation and mill near Mississagi in 1948. They hoped to cut over one million board feet of lumber at their mill.*

1-42 *Teddy de Lamorandière dressing fish at Killarney, 1949. The commercial fishing of lake trout and whitefish on north Georgian Bay provided a livelihood for many in the town, which is home to a population of mixed Irish and French descent.*

1-40

1-41

1-42

1-43 *Gladys Clements of Elk Lake was the only woman mining recorder in the Montreal River division of the Department of Mines in 1950.*

1-44 *Lunch time in the mechanical-welfare room at the Algoma Steel plant in Sault Ste. Marie, 1952.*

1-45 *Bush pilots must be prepared to fix anything anywhere. This OCN Lands and Forests Beaver had to make a forced landing in the Quetico area in 1950. The old engine was dismantled; a new one was flown in from Sault Ste. Marie and installed on the spot.*

1-43

1-44

1-45

1-46 *Many stories about the growth of the north are not recorded, but they still exist in the memories of oldtimers like these retired bushworkers from Aubrey Falls. Conversations with long-time residents provide a gold mine of historical information.*

1-47 *An awareness of "multiculturalism" has encouraged many ethnic groups to demonstrate their unique traditions with special pride. Certain art forms come to symbolize the tradition as a whole; in the Ukrainian tradition elaborately decorated Easter eggs are given as gifts. These young women practised the old decorating art in Sudbury in 1967.*

1-46

1-47

CHAPTER TWO

Exploration and the Fur Trade

PHILIP ALBANESE
*Thunder Bay, now retired,
has taught History and Geography
in a number of Lakehead schools and in Orillia.*

2-1 *Expressly forbidden to do so by the fur
companies, the* voyageurs *took great delight
in running dangerous rapids. These men are
running a loaded canoe down the Missinaibi
River to Moose Factory. The* avant *(bow
man) and* gouvernail *(steersman) are
standing, while the* milieux *await
instructions either to brake or to apply more
speed.*

2–2

2–3

2-2 Frances Ann Hopkins, a painter and the wife of a Hudson's Bay Co. official, accompanied her husband on his western journies in the 1860s and '70s. In her painting "Canoe Manned by Voyageurs" the artist and her husband are travelling in a canot de maître. The crew appear to be French Canadian, Indian, and Métis voyageurs. The feathered cap marks un hivernant, a man who has travelled west of Fort William and overwintered in the north.

2-3 The York Boat was poled by a crew of 8 to 10 men and designed for heavy transport. It was so heavy it had to be hauled over portages on rollers. These are docked at Nipigon House.

2-4 These young Sturgeon Falls trappers in the 1920s specialized in muskrat, raccoon, fox, and skunk. By this time beaver had almost

disappeared from Northern Ontario. Beaver trapping was forbidden until 1932, when a government program to restock beaver was successful enough to allow trappers to take ten beaver each.

2-5 Trappers at Blind River in the 1930s. Dog teams were popular in the trade; some trappers even devised boots for the dogs, so that the ice would not cut the pads of their feet.

2-4

2-5

2–6 *The Hudson's Bay Co. post at Michipicoten, 1880. Michipicoten replaced Fort William as the major fur-trade centre after the union of the Hudson's Bay and North West companies in 1821.*

2–6

Europen exploration of the area we now call Northern Ontario began in the early 17th century. In 1615 Huron canoes carried Samuel de Champlain, and perhaps Etienne Brûlé, up the Mattawa River, across Lake Nipissing, and down the French River to Georgian Bay. This was probably the first time white explorers had set eyes on the territory. Later this waterway became part of the great Canadian canoe route to the west.

The early French and English explorers of the north searched for a shorter trade route to the Pacific Ocean and Asia. By mid-century it had become clear that no easy route to Asia existed, but there was some compensation: the land was rich in furs. Northern Ontario was a treasure trove of beaver, marten, fox, wolf, and "musquash" or muskrat. The intruders left the dream of Cathay behind and focused on the treasures at hand.

The Indians were the first to harvest the furs. They had hunted and trapped animals for food, clothing, and utensils for thousands of years before European traders appeared on the scene. The Europeans arrived at a time of increasing demand for furs in Europe, especially for the beaver pelts needed by hatmakers. The beaver(felt) hat remained fashionable until the silk hat began to replace it in the 1840s.

While furs were in demand in Europe the Indian tribes in turn provided a market for European manufactured goods—guns and ammunition; knives, axes, needles, and awls; copper and iron kettles; and cloth of all kinds. These useful articles reduced the daily drudgery of a subsistence way of life. A superior technology was eagerly welcomed; as one Indian said, "The beaver does everything well. It makes kettles, hatchets, swords, knives, bread. In short it makes everything.... The English have no sense. They give us twenty knives for one beaver skin." But the trade had its negative side too. It brought an increasing dependency on trade goods, as the Indians lost their traditional skills and way of life. Worse than this, it brought the ravages of liquor and disease.

The Indian was important to the European trader not only as a supplier of furs and consumer of goods, but also as an active participant in the daily routine of the trade. Indians were the traders' guides and interpreters. They made the canoes, toboggans, and snowshoes that were the essential means of transport at the time. The marriages of Indian women with the white traders were perhaps the most obvious symbols of the new alliance.

The Huron of the Georgian Bay area were the early middlemen in the trade between the French and the northern tribes. As early as the 1640s the upper Great Lakes began to fall into the orbit of the fur trade of New France. The destruction of the Huron Nation by the Iroquois in the late 1640s changed the fur-trade patterns: furs were now moved eastward along both shores of Lake Superior, with a number of Algonkian-speaking tribes, including the Ojibwa, acting as middlemen. Many of the Ojibwa at this time lived near the southeastern shores of Lake

Superior and the north shore of Lake Huron. They were soon to be replaced as the middlemen of the trade by the French traders themselves.

Pierre Esprit Radisson and Médard Chouart, Sieur des Groseilliers are the first white traders known to have reached the western end of Lake Superior. They wintered at Chequamegon Bay during 1659–60 and crossed the lake in the spring to a point possibly near the Pigeon River, where they met some Crees and Assiniboines. Radisson later claimed that he had reached the northern sea (Hudson Bay), although this claim has been disputed by most historians. More likely he was told by the Indians of a water connection with the bay and realized that the rich fur grounds of the north might be more easily reached by ocean vessel than by canoe.

When Radisson and Groseilliers returned to New France with a rich cargo of furs, they were roughly handled by the authorities. They eventually decided to go to London with their proposal and found a receptive audience there. A trading venture by the *Nonsuch* to James Bay in 1668-69, with Groseilliers aboard, was very successful, and in 1670 the Hudson's Bay Company (HBC) was given a royal charter and a trading monopoly in the Hudson Bay watershed. This vast area included most of what is now Northern Ontario.

Meanwhile other French explorers, traders, and missionaries were beginning to put the Great Lakes region on the map. In 1671 the Sieur de St. Lusson assembled fourteen tribes in council at Sault Ste. Marie and raised the royal arms of France. No doubt the Indians were more impressed with the ceremony of the occasion than they were with its implications. Shortly afterward, while René-Robert Cavelier, Sieur de La Salle, was exploring the lower Mississippi River, Daniel Greysolon, Sieur de Du Lhut, extended his explorations of its upper waters to the north shore of Lake Superior. He built the first posts on the Kaministikwia (Kam) River and on Lake Nipigon in 1679. Soon French traders were siphoning furs that otherwise would have gone to the HBC's bayshore posts in Cree canoes. From the post on the Kam other explorers ventured west, perhaps as far as the present site of Kenora.

France was at war with England during most of the years between 1686 and 1713, and the French used the occasion to mount a seaward challenge to the bayside posts. One expedition by De Troyes and Le Moyne made a spectacular overland journey along the Ottawa and Abitibi rivers in 1686 to capture Moose Factory. From a post on Lake Abitibi the French traders were able to challenge the HBC across the height-of-land. With the bay under their control for most of these years, there was no need for the French to push north and west of Lake Superior. The posts in that region fell into neglect.

France gave up the captured bay posts in 1713 under the Treaty of Utrecht and once more directed its attention to the Lake Superior and Mississippi River regions. A second post was built on the Kam in 1717, and other Lake Superior posts were established (or re-established) under the label of *Les Postes du Nord*. HBC officers once again began to report the activities of the "interloping" *coureurs de bois*.

Among the French post commanders in the 1720s, Pierre La Vérendrye deserves the most attention. While posted at Nipigon, he was given a rough map drawn by an Indian named Ochagach. It showed a water connection with the west and hinted at a western sea. Part of the route west of Lake Superior had already been explored, and the Grande Portage of the Pigeon River was known to French traders by that time. It soon became a viable alternative to the longer and more difficult Kam route.

By 1731 La Vérendrye was ready to enter the western interior. Fort Michilimackinac and Fort Kam were the main dispatch posts, but others were established—Fort St. Pierre (now Fort Frances) and Fort St. Charles (near today's Kenora). For the next five years the activities of La Vérendrye and his sons focused on these posts. Since the costs of their exploration were paid by the profits of the trade, it was important for them to be on friendly terms with the neighbouring Crees and Monsoni. In doing so, the La Vérendryes took their side against the Sioux. Although La Vérendrye preferred to have all the tribes at

2-7 *Samuel de Champlain, Etienne Brûlé, and the Hurons on Lake Nipissing, 1615. This bronze plaque is one of four created by Hans Wiemer in 1980 to commemorate the early exploration of the area.*

2-8 *At the other end of the social and commercial scale from the voyageurs were men like Simon McTavish. He shared in the organization of the North West Co. in 1779 and by 1787 was the senior partner. He* made many summer trips to the Rendezvous at Grand Portage, and the company prospered under his leadership. He died, one of the richest men in Montreal, in 1804.

2-9 *This French illustration of 1754 contains two maps. The map at the bottom shows* Terres Angloises *bordering on* Baye de Hudson, *while* Nouvelle France *occupies almost all of the rest of the northern* half of the continent. The map at the top is a cleaned-up version of a 1729 map of the route between Lake Superior and Lake Winnipeg. The original map was drawn by La Verendrye's Indian guide, Ochagach, in the hope that it would eventually lead La Verendrye to manes de pierres brilliantes ("mountains of shining stones") in the west.

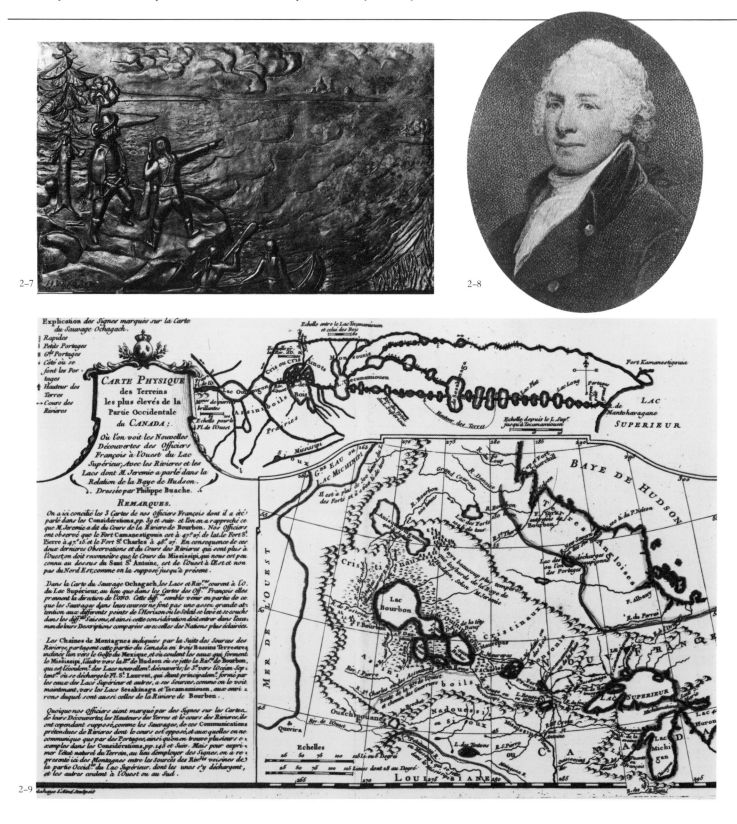

2-7

2-8

2-9

2–10

2–11

2–12

2-10 *In 1871 the Hudson's Bay Co. chief factors included Donald A. Smith, later Lord Strathcona (second from left). Smith was responsible for negotiating the transfer of Rupert's Land to Canada, risked his personal fortune to finance the Canadian Pacific Railway, and was the largest shareholder of the Bank of Montreal—all while governor of the Hudson's Bay Co.*

2-11 *The Hudson's Bay Co. first entered the fur trade in the 1670s in ships, rather than canoes. Vessels like the* Lady Head II *brought supplies to the bayside posts of Fort Albany and Moose Factory and took furs back to England in lots larger than could be managed on inland waters.*

2-12 *Freight canoes, smaller than the* canot de maître, *were lighter to carry and more manoeuvrable in rapids. New Brunswick House, 1903.*

peace with one another, this was not to be: the Indians were drawn into the French-English struggle for control of the trade.

While the La Vérendryes continued their western exploration and trade with the Crees and Assiniboines, others traded at such posts as Temiskaming, Michipicoten, Nipigon, and Kaministikwia. Competition with the HBC was severe in the James Bay watershed, where Moose Factory and Fort Albany did a large business. Transportation costs were a problem for both areas. Michilimackinac became an important supply depot for the French traders, while HBC employees were encouraged to hunt and fish for their own sustenance or to buy food from their Cree neighbours. Competition from the French forced the HBC up the Albany River as early as 1720, and led them to offer more for furs in the southern parts of Rupert's Land.

In 1755 Britain and France were once again at war, and French officers were recalled from the fur-trade posts for military duty. The French traders who returned to Canada after the British conquest of 1759-60 were now subject to the British authorities. Though the fur trade was now entirely under British control, French Canadians continued to be involved, some as merchants and outfitters but most as *voyageurs*. Their knowledge of the land and its inhabitants, of the waterways, and of the mechanics of the trade were vital to the success of their new employers, the Anglo-American and Scottish merchants of Montreal. These merchants and wintering partners, or *bourgeois* as they preferred to call themselves, came to depend on French Canadian *engagés* to provide the day-to-day labour.

Many of these Montreal traders began their operations as individuals or partnerships. Strong competition eventually forced them to form larger associations allied with Montreal merchant houses. The largest of these, organized in 1779, was the North West Company (NWC). By 1800 it had overtaken the HBC in the volume of furs produced. Michilimackinac was the main advance depot of the Montreal traders, as it had been during the French period. Grand Portage assumed this role when the *Rendezvous* system was perfected by the NWC. The post at Lac La Pluie was established as the depot for the Athabasca brigades, for that district was too far away for the wintering partners there to reach Grand Portage and return before freeze-up. They solved this problem by leaving their furs at Lac La Pluie and travelling to Grand Portage in a light canoe to take part in the meeting.

The peace treaty signed in 1783 between Britain and the United States put Grand Portage within American territory. Accordingly in 1784 NWC officials sent Edward Umfreville to explore a new route from Lake Superior to the western interior, the Kam route being unknown to them at the time. Umfreville started from Lake Nipigon and reached the Winnipeg River by way of the English River system. Though the route was adequate for local use, it proved too long and difficult to serve as a link in the trunk canoe route. Fortunately Roderick MacKenzie rediscovered the Kam route in 1798. Construction of a new post on the Kam began a few years later, and the first *Rendezvous* was held there in 1803.

Along the way Umfreville may have met HBC traders or have heard of their activities. No longer content to sit in their posts on the bay while furs meant for them were being intercepted by "pedlars from Quebec" who were often as thick as "muskettos," HBC officers began to send parties inland to establish new posts. Henley House, Gloucester House, Martin Falls, and Osnaburgh House were built on the Albany River in succession from 1744 to 1786. Other posts followed at Lac Seul, Red Lake, Sturgeon Lake, and Nipigon. The NWC, not resting on their paddles, proceeded to match the HBC post-for-post. The HBC was equally aggressive in the Moose-Missinaibi watershed and built posts at Frederick House, Brunswick House, and elsewhere to counter the NWC threat from the forts at Abitibi and Temiskaming.

This southern expansion of the HBC occurred while many of the Montreal traders were still active south and west of the Great Lakes, in American territory. Pressure from the American authorities, coupled with the attraction of richer fur areas to the northwest, gradually induced many of them to shift their ground. Many joined the NWC, while others organized the New North West Company, known as the XY Company, in 1798. Alexander Mackenzie joined this company after a falling-out with Simon McTavish, chief director of the NWC, in 1799. At issue was the future conduct of the trade.

Three years after the split Mackenzie published his *Voyages from Montreal...*, in which he suggested that the fur trade in British North America be placed under Imperial auspices so that it could expand across the Rocky Mountains to the Pacific. Both Napoleon and President Thomas Jefferson obtained copies of the book and made careful notes, but the British government remained indifferent. Mackenzie argued that the NWC should be allowed to use the shorter sea route to Hudson Bay, offsetting the disadvantage of its long canoe route to Montreal. The NWC favoured the proposal, but the HBC understandably refused to grant this concession. Since it appears that McTavish had supported this idea, his falling-out with Mackenzie likely concerned the tactics to be employed in dealing with the HBC.

Despite the disadvantage of a long canoe route, the enterprising NWC was able to hold its own against the English company as well as the XY Company during six years of keen competition. McTavish's death in 1804 paved the way for the merger of the two North West companies, and the renewed NWC provided stiff competition for the HBC. This was the situation until 1810, when a number of events put the Canadian company at a serious disadvantage.

Perhaps the most serious development was the Earl of Selkirk's plan to establish a colony at Red River, a plan that received the blessing of the HBC in 1811. The large land grant lay astride the NWC canoe route and in the middle of the buffalo grounds that supplied the pemmican to fuel the canoe brigades. NWC employees destroyed the Red River Colony twice, in 1815 and 1816. The second destruction, highlighted by the massacre of the governor and twenty settlers at Seven Oaks, had serious consequences for the NWC. Selkirk and his men seized Fort William and other NWC posts.

When news of the conflict reached officials in Canada and London, they took immediate action by sending commissioners west to re-establish law and order. Selkirk was forced to restore the captured posts—Fort William, Lac La Pluie, Michipicoten, Pic, and Fond du Lac (Duluth)—to the NWC. With the commissioners' report in hand, Selkirk and the NWC took their cases to the courts in Canada. The litigation that followed was long and costly, destroying the personal fortunes of both Selkirk and William McGillivray.

Despite the courts and the Prince Regent's proclamation urging the two parties to keep the peace, the conflict continued. Though the HBC suffered greater losses, it was in a better financial position to sustain them than was the NWC, which began to show signs of strain. At the 1819 *Rendezvous* the wintering partners of the NWC refused to renew the partnership agreement. Eighteen of them began secret negotiations with the HBC in London. By 1820 William and Simon McGillivray had seen the writing on the wall.

Union of some kind appeared to be the only alternative to ruin for both companies. Since the HBC was the less battered of the two companies, it was in a stronger negotiating position and made the most of it. The NWC was simply absorbed into the HBC. "This is not amalgamation, it is submersion. We are drowned Men," exclaimed one of the partners. Actually they came off quite well, obtaining most of the commissioned ranks in the reorganized company, and later they served the HBC with distinction. The 1821 *Rendezvous* at Fort William was the last.

Fort William was replaced as the inland headquarters by York Factory and Norway House, and most goods and furs would now move through the bay route, the transit route that the NWC had sought years before. Yet Fort William did not altogether disappear from the fur-trade map, for local trade continued as before, and HBC brigades still continued to use the trunk route. For most of the forty years from 1820 to 1860 Governor Simpson passed through Fort William on his annual inspection trip of company posts.

2-13

2-14

Fort William remained the headquarters of the Lake Superior district until 1827, when that minor distinction was lost to Michipicoten. Furs from the Lake Superior district were now shipped through Michipicoten and overland to Moose Factory, still a major seaport for the HBC. Though most of the trade goods came from Britain, those from Canada continued to pass through Fort William along the canoe route. Schooner service between Sault Ste. Marie and Fort William, pioneered by the NWC, continued as part of the HBC transport system.

Most Northern Ontario fur-trading posts were maintained after the union of 1821. They continued to serve the needs of the local population, who became more and more dependent on them as time passed. Post journals after 1821 often referred to the depletion of large game and prime fur-bearing animals alike. The HBC made a number of attempts to replenish the beaver supply by restricting hunting, but these measures were only partially successful. As the natives became more and more dependent on small game and fish for food, they faced the threat of starvation when these failed. Disease often accompanied hunger, and there were many reports of the ravages of whooping cough, influenza, and measles.

After 1838 Northern Ontario became an active mission field, first for the Methodists and Roman Catholics and later for the Anglicans. The missionaries were given considerable assistance by the HBC, although Simpson and other company officers had mixed feelings about missionary activity, which was usually associated with the establishment of agricultural communities. They feared that the Indians might be turned away from their traditional way of life. But the company's ruling London Committee was under strong Evangelical influence at the time, and Simpson had to defer to its wishes. The Evangelical influence was also evident in the company's attempt to deal with the liquor problem, long an unfortunate by-product of the fur trade. Attempts to restrict the sale of liquor met with limited success; by that time it had become too firmly entrenched in the trade.

Until the mid-1840s Northern Ontario was made up of two societies, native and fur-trade, dependent on each other and living in relative harmony. By the mid-19th century, however, the advance of industry began to change their relationship. Already, mining companies were appearing on the shores of Georgian Bay and Lake Superior. To prepare the way for them, the government of the Province of Canada negotiated the Robinson-Superior Treaty with Ojibwa chiefs at Sault Ste. Marie in 1850. By this treaty the chiefs surrendered land along the north shore of Lake Superior in exchange for land reserves, cash payments, and annual subsidies. In a similar treaty a few days later, the Robinson-Huron Treaty, other chiefs surrendered their lands along Georgian Bay and Lake Huron.

In 1855, the year John McIntyre took charge of the post at Fort William, the United States government opened the Soo canal, making possible the easy passage of large vessels to and from Lake Superior. Also about this time, agrarian and commercial interest groups began to lobby the government to annex the west. In Britain the HBC's monopoly was also under attack. Rupert's Land was becoming too valuable to be left in the hands of fur traders; the land was ripe for settlement and commercial development. There was also some fear that if Canada did not claim the west, the United States might take it over.

The fur trade in Northwestern Ontario was soon overshadowed by the Dawson Road, the Canadian Pacific Railway, mining, logging, and settlement. Resource development, especially logging, was making inroads into Northeastern Ontario. The fur trade was no longer the leading edge of history around the Great Lakes; the old order was giving way.

In 1860 George Simpson, still the governor of the HBC, died in Montreal. His passing marked the end of the fur trade as the major economic force in the vast interior. But the fur trade remained a viable economic enterprise in Northern Ontario and in Canada's north, as it still is today. It is no longer the mainstay of the economy; that role has been taken by forestry, mining, and transportation. But in many small communities the trading post is still the centre of business life and a reminder of past times.

2-15 *The John McIntyre family relaxing on their front porch at Fort William, about 1860. McIntyre was in charge of the Hudson's Bay Co.'s post at Fort William from 1855 to 1870.*

2-16 *Traders, clerks, factors, and post operators were the middlemen in the fur trade. With the formation of the trading companies came the bourgeois, each of whom had a share in the business. By the 1870s, when this picture of Fort William was taken, most of the French traders and operators had been replaced by Scots. The cannons at the gateway now grace Thunder Bay City*

Hall, a legacy from John McIntyre's daughter, Annie. In the background is the McIntyre residence.

2-15

2-16

2–17 *This 1857 drawing by John Fleming shows Fort William 50 years after its grandest days, when the site had 23 acres of buildings and 357 acres under cultivation. The fort had shrunk to about 13 acres by 1857; the Great Hall had been dismantled in 1850.*

2–18 *This 1873 view of Prince Arthur's Landing from Fort William shows the encampment outside the fort. Strict segregation was the rule at trading posts. Voyageurs and even the native wives and families of company officials encamped outside the 15-foot walls of the fort. Pen-and-ink drawing by William Armstrong, watercoloured by B. Kroupa.*

2–17

2–18

2-19 *Built in 1810, the stone-block powder magazine was all that remained of Fort William in 1890. It is surrounded by the CPR's expanding freight yards, which eventually led to the building's demolition. Archaeologists have recently completed a project to retrieve fur-trade history from the ground between the tracks.*

2-19

2-20 *This 1869 view of Moose Factory provides some insight into post life on the bays. A bell tower announced the arrival of ships; the docks would accommodate an 8-foot tide, and wooden sidewalks were for high-water conditions. Roof ladders were for fire protection, and fences kept grazing livestock out of the gardens. Cannons below the tower once unsuccessfully guarded the post.*

2-21 *The Hudson's Bay Co. encouraged*
2-22 *gardening and livestock-keeping at its posts. The garden greens supplemented the heavy protein diet and prevented scurvy. Local produce also reduced the heavy bill for imported supplies. Unfortunately, neither the Europeans nor the natives knew much about gardening, and it was often an uphill struggle. 2-21 shows small backyard gardens, fenced to keep out livestock, at Moose Factory about 1890. In 2-22 Indian women hill-up potatoes at New Brunswick House in 1903.*

2-20

2-21

2-22

2–23 *Revillon Frères was begun by Victor Revillon, a Parisian who inherited a fur business in 1835. In 1839 he acquired a firm established in 1723. Revillon incorporated in Canada in 1904 and located its main depot on Strutton Island in James Bay. Hudson's Bay Co. and Revillon posts were often found together in the smaller settlements, and the HBC acquired Revillon in 1936. This is the Revillon Bros. store at Nipigon in 1910.*

2–24 *An Ojibwa camp with trade kettles near the Lake of the Woods, early 1900s. Kettles were only one of many popular trade items among the fur traders.*

2–25 *Clothing and firearms were also important trade goods. The residents of this Indian village at Nipigon in 1888 adopted European styles of dress.*

2–23

2–24

2–25

2-26 *Indian women were a vital link in the fur trade. They skinned the animals, dressed the furs, made snowshoes, clothing, and footwear, and often carried the bundles of furs to the post. This Ojibwa woman at New Brunswick House in 1910 is making a fishnet.*

2-27 *Perhaps Indian women benefited most from trade goods. Steel kettles, needles and thread, and in this case a sewing machine made life a little easier. This portrait was taken at the Hudson's Bay Co. post at Abitibi in 1905.*

2–26

2–27

2-28 *Traditionally beaver were caught by blockading them inside their lodges, which were then broken open with poles. Here a steel-frame spring trap is being set at the entrance to a lodge above the ice surface of James Bay. The stakes will guide the beaver into the trap.*

2-29 *Mr. T. Taylor trapped beaver in the*
2-30 *Mammamattawa area in 1948. In 2-29 he inspects the trap before setting it; in 2-30 he displays the fruits of his labours.*

2-31 *Bob McColl and Maggie Muir took these furs near Hymers, in the Kakabeka Falls area, in the 1920s. The pelts in the background are parchment beaver, stretched on a hoop and sun-dried, leaving the inside skin clean and white. These would be used for coats. An otter is turned inside-out and stretched on a board to dry.*

2-28

2-29

2-30

2-31

45

2–32 *The making of parchment beaver has*
2–33 *remained unchanged over the past century.*
The pelt is separated from the fatty
underlayer with a blunt bone tool, here done
by a Michipicoten Island couple in 1961 (2-
32). Springy willow and alder are shaped
into hoops, and the beaver pelt is sewn inside
the frame. Then the fat and flesh are scraped
off, and the parchment surface is dried in the
sun (2-33).

2–32

2–33

2-34 *The trading post's role as "store" brought*
2-35 *the outside world into the north. The
Europeans initially set an official rate of
exchange, which the Indians were reluctant
to change. When factors attempted to supply
a short measure in cloth or powder, native*

*traders refused the trade. In 2-34, muskrat
and beaver skins are inspected at
Mammattawa in 1948. In 2-35, Mrs.
Morris Oliver brings her furs to the
Hudson's Bay Co. agent Mallard in
Hornepayne in 1958.*

2-36 *These boys at the Nipigon House post in
1908 appear to be passing the time rather
than trading. In the early days of the trade
native people were not allowed into the
"store"; they dealt with white traders outside
the post or through a window.*

2-34

2-35

2-36

2-37 *Fur packing at Fort Albany, 1941. Eddie Ferriers and K. Rettalick inspect the pelts.*

2-38 *Simcoe Scott and Bill Louttit press fur bales at Fort Albany in the 1930s.*

2-37

2-38

CHAPTER THREE

Transportation and Communications

ERNIE EPP
*Associate Professor of History,
Lakehead University,
Thunder Bay.*

3-1 *By 1885 the canals at Sault Ste. Marie were
large enough to allow ships the size of the
SS Sarnian to pass.*

3-2 In 1868 construction began on the 45-mile Dawson Road from Port Arthur to Lake Shebandowan, part of a 451-mile road to the Red River settlement. This pen-and-ink drawing by William Armstrong in 1872 shows the station at the head of Lake Shebandowan. The road was abandoned in favour of the proposed railway in 1878.

3-3 The St. Marys Rapids were a navigation hazard until the first American lock opened in 1855. This photo shows the last stone being laid in the construction of the Canadian locks in 1895.

3-4 A new horse and buggy were a sure sign that a bachelor was ready, and financially able, to get married. While trying to appear nonchalant, this fellow is keeping a very tight rein on his snappy new "driver." Gore Bay, about 1910.

3-5 The Mattagami wagon road at Timmins, about 1911. Layers of logs were sunk into the mud to form a corduroy road.

3-2

3-3

3-4

3-5

3-6 Northern Ontario roads could be treacherous in both winter and summer. This truck is stuck on the road to the Bankfield Mine near Geraldton, around 1937.

3-7 Things didn't always run smoothly in either
3-8 the construction or operation of the railways. In 3-7, Canadian Northern Railway locomotive No. 10 jumped the track in the Fort Frances district in 1902. In 3-8, the CPR Canadian was wrecked east of Schreiber in 1965, when a flash flood washed out part of the track.

3-6

3-7

3-8

Northern Ontario's vast area of trees and lakes, rock and rivers presents a formidable barrier to the traveller. Until the mid-19th century the main methods of long-distance travel were those developed by the Algonkians and adopted by the Europeans: walking and canoeing in the summer, and snowshoeing and toboganning in the winter. Sometimes dog teams were used to pull heavy loads and quicken the journey.

For thousands of years the light but sturdy birchbark canoe enabled the Algonkians to follow the lakes and rivers that drained into the Great Lakes, Hudson Bay, and James Bay. Some of the Nipissing Algonkians travelled to Sault Ste. Marie in winter to trade with hunters who lived around Lake Michigan and Lake Superior. They made spring journeys to trade on Hudson Bay or James Bay, and the furs they obtained there were brought to the market at Montreal. In the fall the Nipissings carried dried fish south to the Hurons and traded it for corn, one of their winter foods.

Later, canoes provided the transport basis of prosperity for the people of the St. Lawrence valley. During 150 years of trade out of Montreal, thousands of tons of goods were transported west, and thousands of tons of well-packed furs started back toward the markets of the Old World. The canoes also carried the letters and dispatches that, with the memories of the traders, provided the communications of a far-flung empire.

"Birch-rind" canoes also enabled Cree traders to deal with Hudson's Bay Company factors from 1670 to 1774, when the company traded at the bay. When its servants established posts in the interior they too used canoes, constructing their own when the Cree traders would not sell them. Eventually the company extended its transportation advantage on the inland bays by using freight boats on the rivers draining into the bays. These boats remained in service on the Albany and Severn rivers until almost the middle of the 20th century.

The first ship to sail on the Great Lakes was built in 1679. René-Robert Cavelier, Sieur de la Salle, ordered the construction of a small sailing ship to carry freight between Niagara and Lake Michigan. *Le Griffon* arrived safely at its Green Bay destination, but was lost on the return voyage. The experiment was not repeated for another century, when the NWC began to use sailing vessels on the Great Lakes.

Steam-powered ships began to sail the upper Great Lakes soon afterward. The *Gore* made its first run between Sturgeon Bay and Sault Ste. Marie in 1838. In the 1840s steam-powered ships were used by prospectors and miners in Northern Ontario; the *Bruce Mines* was one of the ships that stopped at ports on Georgian Bay and in the North Channel of Lake Huron. The St. Marys Rapids had been bypassed by a canal in 1798, but the canal was only large enough to allow the North West Company's canoes to pass Sault Ste. Marie. Later, steam-powered vessels were dragged past the rapids to enter the trade across Lake Superior.

The modern era of transportation on the upper Great Lakes began in 1855, when the first Soo canal was built by American interests on the Michigan side of the international boundary. A canal-sized vessel could now make the voyage from Montreal or from other St. Lawrence ports all the way to the Lakehead without having to transship cargo at any point.

Toronto's interest in the British Northwest was encouraged in the same year by completion of the Northern Railway from Toronto to Collingwood. In 1858 Torontonians established a North West Transportation, Navigation and Railway Company and obtained the Post Office contract to carry mail to the Lakehead and beyond. These Torontonians dreamed of building rail lines from Lake Superior to Rainy Lake and from the Lake of the Woods to Red River. Steamers on Rainy Lake, Rainy River, and the Lake of the Woods would carry passengers and freight from one rail line to the other.

As interest in the northwest grew in the Province of Canada during the 1860s, these possibilities began to interest the Canadian government. The *Algoma* came into service in 1865, sailing out of Collingwood and serving Lake Huron's North Channel ports and the Lake Superior trade as far as the Landing on Thunder Bay. When in 1870 public opinion demanded a military expedition to the new Province of Manitoba to end the Red River Resistance, the *Algoma* carried part of Colonel Garnet Wolseley's force to Prince Arthur's Landing (as he named the site) and the Dawson Road to the west.

George M. Grant's account of the 1872 "Ocean to Ocean" journey revealed how the overland route to Manitoba was being improved. Wagons were available on the road segments, staging houses had been established to shelter travellers, and steamers easily towed barges and flotillas of canoes to the last overland section. But the route remained far more difficult than the American railway route beyond Duluth.

American competition led the Canadian government to offer British Columbia a railway in 1871 and to promise completion of it within ten years. Grant's journey was in fact the reconnaissance by Sandford Fleming, engineer-in-chief for the Canadian government, of a transcontinental railway route. However, construction of the Intercolonial Railway to the Maritimes occupied the government until 1876, and the Pacific Scandal in 1873 and economic depression slowed work on the Pacific Railway.

Little progress was made during the Mackenzie government's five years of power from 1873 to 1878, although contracts were let in 1875 for railway construction between the Lakehead and the Red River settlement. Five years later, halfway through the first term of Sir John A. Macdonald's National Policy government, almost half of the line remained under construction.

Finally, in the early 1880s, the Canadian government's determination to build an all-Canadian railway was realized. A group of Montrealers was awarded the contract as the Canadian Pacific Railway Company (CPR). The CPR directors first considered routing the railway from Sault Ste. Marie, Michigan, to St. Paul, Minnesota, where there was already a rail connection to Selkirk, Manitoba. By early 1882, however, the CPR had recognized the government's determination to see the main line built north of Lake Superior. Construction westward from Callander and eastward from Fort William began in 1883.

The decision to build an all-Canadian transcontinental railway was one of the most important decisions ever made in Northern Ontario transportation. Much of Northern Ontario could have been bypassed in favour of easier routes, but the all-Canadian route meant that Northern Ontario communities would receive the direct benefits of the railway. The CPR construction through Northern Ontario opened parts of the province that earlier had been travelled only by canoe or on foot, and the mineral discoveries at Sudbury illustrated the value of the line that ran northwest from Sudbury to the shores of Lake Superior at Heron Bay.

The route, completed at high cost in May 1885, had already demonstrated its national importance. The force sent to suppress the North West Rebellion had travelled along the Northern Ontario line, being carried by horse-drawn sleighs on the incomplete sections. Meanwhile, the

3-9 *A birchbark canoe being constructed at Mattice Lake, near Sioux Lookout, in the 1920s. Men usually gathered the materials, cut the bark, and shaped the internal reinforcements. Women did the stitching and decorating.*

3-10 *The harbour at Little Current, Manitoulin Island, in 1874. This was one of the stops for boats travelling from Owen Sound to the Lakehead.*

3-9

3-10

3-11 *The Port Arthur & Silver Islet Royal Mail sled, 1876. Overland carriers such as this one provided the Lakehead's only mail service during the winter.*

3-12 *The women who worked in the Cobalt mailroom in 1907 are identified only as Lyons, Copps, Copps, McKenzie, and Duffy. Fred Presley, far right, was probably the supervisor.*

3-13 *Captain George Purvis with his mail sleigh in front of Gore Bay's hotel, the Ocean House, about 1910. On January 3, 1910, the* Manitoulin Recorder *noted that "the ice bridge is now complete across the channel...in all probability the mail will arrive regularly until the spring break up."*

3-11

3-12

3-13

CPR had in 1883 acquired control of the Toronto, Grey and Bruce Railway, with a line from Toronto to Owen Sound. Soon, CPR steamships were sailing out of Owen Sound, carrying construction materials for the railway to both Algoma Mills and the Lakehead and reducing construction costs. The CPR steamers also joined in the general freight and passenger business on the upper Great Lakes.

The CPR's determination to control Great Lakes traffic led to other important decisions. The company acquired an American railway that ran west from Sault Ste. Marie, Michigan, and then completed its line from Algoma Mills to Sault Ste. Marie in 1888. This branch linked one more Northern Ontario community to the national railway network. In 1889 it was connected by a bridge across the St. Marys River to the Soo line, and the alternative American route to the west became a reality.

These new CPR lines did much more (and less) than link new regions to national markets. Wheat from the prairies mostly left the Lakehead in Great Lakes steamers. A large passenger and package-freight business was handled by the CPR ships and other vessels that eventually became the Northern Navigation Company and was transformed into the Northern Navigation division of Canada Steamship Lines in 1913. The Northern Ontario line of the CPR really came into its own during the winter months, when steamers were unable to run on the Lakes.

The telegraph lines required for the safe and efficient operation of the railway enabled messages to be sent rapidly to and from the Northern Ontario communities located on the CPR lines. Telegraphic dispatches published in Northern Ontario newspapers began to end the sense of frontier isolation that had once clung to these towns. During World War I these newspapers benefited from the federal government's subsidy of the fledgling Canadian Press.

In the mid-1890s two contractors, William Mackenzie and Donald Mann, built a small railway line in western Manitoba. Their Canadian Northern Railway, as they named it in 1898, was eventually linked to the Lakehead through northern Minnesota. By 1902 the Canadian Northern was carrying western grain to Port Arthur.

Increasing western grain production and the desire to profit from it resulted in intense competition among the Canadian Northern, Canadian Pacific, and Grand Trunk railways. In 1902 the Grand Trunk decided to build a transcontinental line of its own. Its acquisition of the Canada Atlantic Railway line from Montreal to Georgian Bay forced the Canadian Northern to acquire other lines and rights in the east and eventually to build a Northern Ontario line of its own between 1911 and 1914.

The Grand Trunk plan for a transcontinental line did not receive government support until 1903. The company was then forced to alter its plans by agreeing to include a government-built National Transcontinental line from Winnipeg through Quebec City to Moncton in its system. This reduced the Grand Trunk Pacific to a line from Winnipeg to Prince Rupert. The Grand Trunk management tried to make a closer connection to its Southern Ontario lines by building a branch from Superior Junction, near Sioux Lookout, to Fort William. This line was opened in 1908, but the National Transcontinental link to Winnipeg was not completed until 1910.

A number of smaller projects during these years opened up Northern Ontario, with varying degrees of success. The 1899 decision of Francis H. Clergue, busy with industrial developments at Sault Ste. Marie, to build a railway north to his iron mines near Michipicoten was successful in the long run. In the short run his Algoma Central and Hudson Bay Railway and Algoma Eastern Railway built only short lines. The first had reached only fifty-five miles north when financial problems in 1903 almost ended the Consolidated Lake Superior enterprises. The second line was little more than a Sudbury mining railway at that time, but between 1907 and 1913 the Algoma Eastern was extended to Little Current on Manitoulin Island. The Algoma Central, which had operated steamships to Michipicoten, extended its rail line to the mines in 1912. It then pushed north to cross the CPR line at Franz and to meet the National Transcontinental line at Hearst in 1914.

The most promising rail development of the time resulted from the passage of the Temiskaming and Northern Ontario Railway Act in 1901. The Ontario government had begun to focus its attention on the agricultural, forest, and mineral potential of the region north of North Bay. A railway could open these territories to Southern Ontario enterprise, as the discovery of silver at Cobalt two years later demonstrated so well. The Temiskaming and Northern Ontario Railway (T & NO) reached New Liskeard by 1905. Construction was then pushed toward the National Transcontinental line at Cochrane, which the T & NO reached in 1908. Branch lines were constructed to the Elk Lake silver fields in 1913, to Timmins and gold in 1912, and to Iroquois Falls and the Abitibi Pulp and Paper mill in 1913. The T & NO had become one of Ontario's greatest development instruments.

By the time the National Transcontinental line across Northern Ontario was completed in 1913, railway technology had opened up rich agricultural, forest, and mineral resources. But large areas of Northwestern Ontario still remained untouched by the transcontinental lines across the southern Canadian Shield. The railways ran no farther north than the 51st parallel, while Northern Ontario stretched to the 56th parallel. It remained for the internal-combustion engine and the aircraft to provide the means of opening these territories.

The peacetime development of aviation began very soon after World War I, as pilots returned from France. As early as 1920 the Ontario government assisted an aerial expedition to James Bay by the Canadian Aero Film Company, which operated out of Remi Lake. The following year, aerial surveys of Northwestern Ontario were conducted from Sioux Lookout. One of these flights turned in a fire report that led to the first firefighting flight in Northern Ontario.

The firefighting problems facing the Ontario Department of Lands and Forests were well illustrated in 1922 by the Haileybury fire. That fire burned two thousand square miles of forest and took forty-four lives. That same year the Ontario government hired Laurentide Air Service Limited of Grand'Mère, Quebec, to provide aerial survey and fire-spotting services. In 1924 the department obtained authority to purchase thirteen Curtiss HS2L flying boats and to inaugurate the Ontario Provincial Air Service.

The Provincial Air Service and the aviation companies that soon appeared provided vital services on the Ontario frontier. When gold was discovered in the Red Lake area in 1925 the Air Service flew in men and mining equipment just before winter. Jack V. Elliott of Hamilton began air services from Hudson to the Red Lake area in March 1926. W. Roy Maxwell, director of the Provincial Air Service from 1924 to 1934, encouraged the organization of Patricia Airways and Exploration at Sioux Lookout the same year. One of his former Air Service pilots, H.A. "Doc" Oaks, flew for Patricia briefly before becoming manager of the new Western Canada Airways. In 1928 Jack Hamell joined Doc Oaks in organizing Northern Aerial Exploration Limited, which provided bush planes to prospectors exploring in remote areas. This company discovered gold deposits at Pickle Lake that same year.

The Red Lake activity led to a number of innovations in transportation and communications. Its importance was indicated by Western Canada Airways' choice of Hudson (and later Sioux Lookout) as its Northern Ontario base. Regular air-mail service was pioneered in the district after skis had been developed that allowed float planes to operate in the winter. The winter movement of heavy freight by tractor-drawn sleighs was also pioneered out of Hudson. Robert W. Starratt's Northern Transportation Company began to provide this service in 1927. This operation was expanded into Starratt Airways and Transportation early in 1935, just in time for the company to share in the largest air-freight contract let in Canada up to that time. The air bases at Hudson and Gold Pines were among the busiest in the world in 1936, when over six hundred tons of equipment were flown to the mines at Casummit Lake.

The construction of airports for a Trans-Canada airway required as much effort in Northern Ontario as in any other part of the country. C.D. Howe's 1937 flight

3-14

3-15

3-16

3-17

3–18 *Modern explorers: with standard, notebook, and a hard-to-manage 66-foot length of chain, these surveyors cut the line for the CPR line near Bluesea Lake almost 300 years after Champlain mapped the area.*

3–19 *Railway construction involved blasting and removing tons of rock. At times it called for roadbeds along shoreline stretches to be filled in, as these men are doing.*

3–18

3–19

across Canada to test the new Trans-Canada Airlines involved stops at Gillies and Sioux Lookout. The first airway developments in Northern Ontario occurred at Kapuskasing and Wagaming, well away from the storms of the Great Lakes as well as the population centres. Not until 1947 were Sault Ste. Marie and Fort William served by Trans-Canada Airlines.

The highway development needed to make automobiles, trucks, and buses important in Northern Ontario transportation was even slower in coming. The Ferguson Highway, opened to Matheson in 1927, gave the eastern edge of Northern Ontario a route to the south of the province. In the following years this highway was extended to Cochrane and beyond, offering an alternative to those served only by the T & NO and northern CNR lines. At the Lakehead, Highway 61, then named the Scott Highway after a Port Arthur lumberman, had been built to the border and linked to a Minnesota highway by a bridge across the Pigeon River in 1917.

The construction of road sections near Northwestern Ontario towns had by the early 1930s contributed only a little toward the completion of a Trans-Canada Highway. A national meeting at Dryden in 1919 led to the organization of a Central Canada Colonization and Highway Association, which continued the struggle others had already launched. Peter Heenan, Liberal MP for Kenora, begged the Bennett government to provide the Ontario government with money to close the gaps between Kenora and Dryden, Fort Frances, and Sioux Lookout. A Trans-Canada Highway from Manitoba to the Lakehead was opened in 1935.

The Ontario government financed Northern Ontario highway construction during the 1930s, but travel remained difficult. By 1944 it was possible to drive Highway 11 beyond the Ferguson Highway to Port Arthur. Northwestern Ontario residents were more likely to take a CPR ferry-steamer from the Lakehead to Sault Ste. Marie. Others drove south into the United States, circled Lake Superior, and rode a ferry back into Canada at Sault Ste. Marie before continuing on to Southern Ontario from there. Highway travel still had far to go when the Canadian government decided in 1949 to aid the construction of a genuine Trans-Canada Highway.

The Ontario section of the Trans-Canada Highway was originally intended to follow the main line of the CPR. This highway would have passed through Chapleau, but the final decision to build the highway north from Sault Ste. Marie opened the entire north shore of Lake Superior to tourist traffic. The decision was a very expensive one, with the 165-mile section between the Agawa River and Marathon costing almost $40 million. After much rock-blasting and bridge-building—no fewer than twenty-five bridges were required—the scenic route was completed in 1960.

The completion of the Trans-Canada Highway and other Northern Ontario highways opened the possibility of truck transport for the forest and mining industries. A provincial mining and access road committee began to consider this option in 1954, and the Ontario government obtained Canadian assistance in 1959 under the Roads to Resources Agreement to build roads north from the Trans-Canada Highway. This program eventually linked Northwestern Ontario communities such as Red Lake and Pickle Lake to the southern centres.

Improvements in the communications systems matched transportation developments. The telephone had been introduced for local use in the developed communities soon after it was invented in the 1870s. By 1909 Fort William and Port Arthur had municipally owned systems comparable to the provincially owned systems on the prairies. The Bell Telephone Company made its regional impact after 1958, when microwave technology allowed the Trans-Canada Telephone System to become a reality. This radio relay system carried not only telephone conversations and other exchanges of data, but also the national networks of the Canadian Broadcasting Corporation and CTV.

Radio broadcasting was the great communications achievement of the years between the wars. The Ontario Forestry Service operated public commercial stations that provided point-to-point radiotelephone and radio-telegraph services as well as ground-to-air radiotele-

3-20 *Grand Trunk Pacific rolling stock carrying ties and rails to the end of the track, in the Thunder Bay area, around 1905. A new spur line is being built.*

phone service for pilots. The CBC, established in 1936, soon had affiliated stations in North Bay, Kirkland Lake, Timmins, Sudbury, and Fort William. Privately owned stations at Sault Ste. Marie and Kenora broadcast CBC material more selectively. This system continued with little change other than the appearance of more privately owned stations until the CBC opened regional production facilities in Sudbury and Thunder Bay.

The Ontario Ministry of Transportation and Communications (MTC) was created in 1971 to shift provincial attention from highway construction to public transportation and communications systems. This was a significant development for the still-isolated communities of Northern Ontario. Also in 1971 the Ontario government established NorOntair to provide a demonstration Short Take-Off and Landing (STOL) program in Northeastern Ontario. When it was extended to Northwestern Ontario in 1975, it was intended to allow travellers to fly to small centres and back home the same day. With expanded Air Canada and Nordair service to the larger cities, this gave Northern Ontario travellers many options they had not had before.

The far northern communities, many of them Indian settlements, also benefited from MTC programs encour-

aged by the Ministry of Northern Affairs. The Remote Airports Program, begun in 1969, advanced rapidly during the 1970s and '80s. Some of the first to benefit were the people of Sandy Lake, Big Trout Lake, Winisk, and Fort Albany. Recently Pikangikum, Fort Hope, Attawapiskat, and Fort Severn have been provided with small airports. Now these communities also have modern telephone service, thanks to microwave systems constructed by Bell Canada in the less distant communities and to Telesat Canada's Anik satellites in the more remote ones. Satellite technology is ending the sense of isolation long felt in northern communities.

Northern Ontarians now have many thoroughly modern transportation and communications systems available to them, while they still use and jealously guard the older systems. Northern communities on the CNR lines are acutely aware of every threat to reduce or cancel the Via Rail operations that make passenger travel and employment possible. The people of Thunder Bay remain anxious about their under-utilized Keefer Terminal, regarded at its opening in 1962 as the crown of the St. Lawrence Seaway. And producers throughout Northern Ontario continue to press for reductions in the cost of moving freight out of the north.

3-20

3-21 This 110-foot-high temporary trestle spanned the Jackfish River in 1911. Temporary trestles were often built during railway construction; permanent bridges were built later, when there was more time and money.

3-22 Where there are machines there have to be maintenance crews. These workers posed with Canadian Northern Railway locomotive 228 at the Rainy River roundhouse, about 1905. The railway runs west through Minnesota to reach Winnipeg.

3-21

3-22

3-23 *Finally the trains got through. This is the first train to visit Golden City in the Porcupine area. It was 1911; a passenger could now board the Temiskaming & Northern Ontario train in Toronto on one day and be in the gold camp the next.*

3-24 *The water-rail combination of transport services has been vital to the economy of Northern Ontario. The rail terminus at Fort William—Port Arthur was the transshipment point for western grain. Today, Thunder Bay is the world's largest grain-handling centre.*

3-23

3-24

3-25 *Aviation development in Northern Ontario was spearheaded by several adventurous young men. This photograph, taken at Nipigon House in 1925, shows H.A. "Doc" Oaks (left), with Hudson's Bay Co. factor Paddy McGuire (with hat), Paddy's son, and air engineers Sandy Sanderson and L.H. Briggs.*

3-26 *An aluminum-skinned Junkers at the Kinneally's Lodge landing, Minnitaki, east of Sioux Lookout, in 1930. The Junkers was like a flying boxcar, with a carrying capacity of over three tons.*

3-25

3-26

3-27 *The crew of the Provincial Air Service at Sioux Lookout Station around 1925, on a Curtiss HS2L flying boat. The H-boat has been called the mother hen of northwest flying machines. It was mainly used for fire spotting.*

3-28 *The De Havilland Otter (left) is still used in northern transport. Its smaller brother, the Beaver (right), is said to be the plane that opened the north, with a large payload for its size. These planes are at the Sioux Lookout docks in 1955.*

3-27

3-28

3-29 *Winter flying demanded adaptations in materials and methods. Here Jack Smith of Sault Ste. Marie is building skis for Beaver aircraft in the 1950s.*

3-30 *Lancaster bomber crews were stationed in North Bay in 1948 to experiment with dry-ice bombing of forest fires. This crew consisted of (standing, left to right): J.E. Johnson, co-pilot; R.B. West, pilot; D.F. Short, engineer; B.L. Russell, navigator; and W.H. Barclay, wireless. Those sitting are J.W. Healey, fitter; and R. Haglund, rigger.*

3-29

3-30

3-31 *August Kinvate's ox cart in turn-of-the-century New Liskeard. This rig is more complex than those usually used for oxen; the horse collar and one-horse shafts replace the yoke.*

3-32 *The inside of S. A. Smith's Carriage and Blacksmith shop, Emo, in 1902. The men are working on Sarven Patented Hub wheels with steel tires. The man at the left is drilling holes for tire bolts; the man in the middle is tightening the nuts on tire bolts.*

3-31

3-32

3-33 *With the development of highway routes and gasoline-powered vehicles came the proliferation of gas and service stations and the organization of bus lines. These Temiskaming Bus Lines vehicles are parked at McGuire's Service Centre, a Ford dealership in New Liskeard, in 1935.*

3-34 *The development of the track vehicle with skis was a breakthrough. This is a 12-seater Chrysler motor product near Longlac in 1946.*

3-35 *Tractor trains could reach communities not served by roads or railways. This tractor is hauling gasoline and building materials through slush on Lac Seul in the 1930s.*

3-33

3-34

3-35

3-36 *Wireless (radio) operators were a crucial link in the Ontario Forestry Service's communication system. Eric Kurt was a wireless operator for the Forestry Branch, probably at Puckasaw Depot, in the 1920s.*

3-37 *The electrical and electronic communications systems kept the transportation system running. Norma Neva and Nora Kettle worked in the CPR telegraph office in Sudbury in 1947.*

3-38 *Telex and radio are part of the Ministry of Natural Resources communications system in Thunder Bay, 1970.*

3-39 *CKSO-TV of Sudbury went on the air in 1953 as the first privately owned television station in Canada. Here, in the early years of programming, Bill Kehoe and Helen Church present a cooking show in front of the station's only camera.*

3-40 *TVOntario provides noncommercial television programming throughout Ontario. Many smaller northern communities have installed a receiving dish through a program supported by the Ministry of Northern Affairs.*

3-36

3-37

3-38

3-39

3-40

CHAPTER FOUR

Lumbering, Pulp and Paper, and Forestry

VICTOR C. SMITH

Assistant Professor of History,
Lakehead University,
Thunder Bay.

4-1 *Brag loads were a form of entertainment, rather than serious logging activity. Camps would challenge each other to see who could stack the most logs. Under the right conditions (about 0°C) this load could be pulled by two horses. The snow under the runners would melt, and the sleigh would run on a thin film of water. Lake Matinenda, around 1930.*

4-2 *Logging at North Bay, around 1913. Some of the white pine trees were almost 6 feet wide and 150 feet high.*

4-3 *A corduroy tote road in the Blind River area in the 1920s. These roads often provided the only access to lumber camps.*

4-2

4-3

4-4 Not all woodsworkers lived in camps, but many lived in camps like this one, operated by the Keewatin Lumbering and Manufacturing Co. in 1901. Camps housed both the lumberjacks and the teamsters, in often-deplorable conditions. The snow on the roofs of the buildings may indicate that they were not heated.

4-5 The Black River Drive at Matheson, around 1915. River drivers were proud of their skills; some claimed to be able to throw a bar of soap into the water and walk to shore on the bubbles.

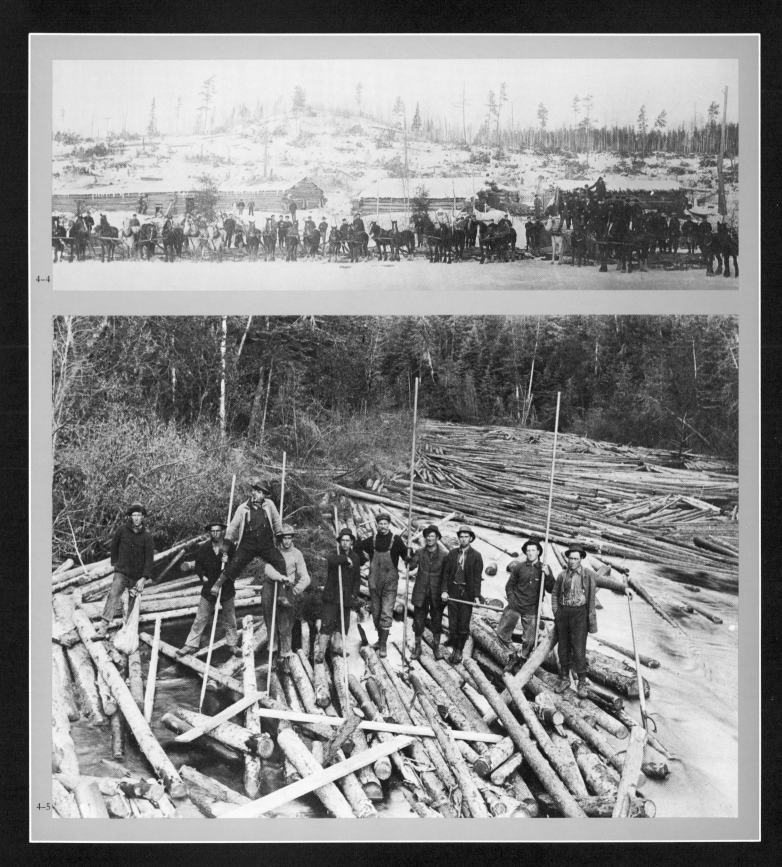

4-4

4-5

4–6 Smaller timber berths or limits were
sometimes worked by family businesses.
The Monahan family worked as a unit near
Matheson around 1910.

4–7 A card game underway in a bunkhouse in
the Rainy River area, early 1900s. Much of
the workers' money went toward alcohol,
tobacco, and gambling, although some
companies forbade all three. Sometimes
employees were charged for room and board,
as well as for clothes and tobacco.
Lumberjacks were known to emerge from the
woods after six months' work, in debt to
their employers.

4–6

4–7

THE FORESTS are a fact of life in Northern Ontario—perhaps even *the* fact of life. Anyone who has travelled across the northern part of the province can easily see that forests dominate the landscape. They have also dominated the history of the region. Long before Europeans came to the area the forests offered fuel and shelter, and the animals of the forests provided food and clothing, for the Ojibwa and Cree.

The first European inhabitants contented themselves with "plugging into" and extending existing fur-trade networks in the 17th and 18th centuries. They disturbed the forests little more than the original inhabitants did. But toward the end of the 19th century the pace, scale, and nature of forest use changed drastically. Farmers and railway builders, miners and hydro engineers, tourists and hunters came to the region, each placing new and different demands on the forests. One group above all made the greatest impact on Northern Ontario's forests—those who sought new supplies of timber, lumber, and pulpwood for rapidly expanding North American markets.

To the traveller driving by them on the highway, most trees look fairly much alike, except in winter, when some remain green (the softwoods) and others lose their leaves (the hardwoods). To those who have lived in and by and with the forests, this distinction is only the beginning. For many reasons softwoods have been regarded as much more valuable than hardwoods in North America, and the Northern Ontario forests contain many important softwoods.

In the southeast, between Sudbury and Sault Ste. Marie, and in the far west, between the head of Lake Superior and the Lake of the Woods, the majestic white and red pines were the first softwoods to be cut in great numbers. In the rest of the region, north as far as James Bay (where the forests become less dense because of poorer soils and a colder climate) the most important softwoods have been white and black spruce. Others such as jack pine, balsam, and hemlock, and even some hardwoods such as white birch and poplar, have been of some importance, but the real prizes have been the white pine and white spruce. These were the "merchantable" trees—the ones most sought after—and until recently the history of the forest industries in Northern Ontario has largely been based on them.

That history can be divided into three overlapping phases. The first two roughly correspond to the periods of the greatest exploitation of the white pine and white spruce. From the 1870s to the early 1900s cutting white pine for timber and lumber was the main forest-based industry. After that time cutting continued, but at a greatly reduced rate. The merchantable stands became fewer, smaller, and harder to find. Around 1900 attention shifted to spruce, partly for lumber, but more especially as raw material for the new giant beginning to appear in Northern Ontario's forests—the pulp-and-paper industry. After World War II a third phase began, one that has continued to this day. It has involved a virtual revolution both in the methods of harvesting trees and in the public's attitudes toward forests. The era of pine was followed by the era of spruce, and both have now been replaced by a new era of forestry.

The era of white pine opened up Northern Ontario's forests in the 1880s. White pine is one of the largest of Eastern Canadian trees, sometimes reaching a height of 200 feet and a diameter of five feet at the base. It was also one of the best—strong enough for ships' masts, adaptable to almost any building purpose, and valuable enough to be transported hundreds of miles and still fetch a profit. Little wonder that in their increasingly desperate search for choice stands of pine in the late 19th century, timber operators came to Northern Ontario from both Canada and the United States. Their activities were influenced by four factors: provincial government policies, the geographical distribution of pine stands, the availability of water transport, and the primacy of American markets.

One of the main aims of provincial land policies at this time was to open up new farming areas in the north. In the minds of politicians this aim was closely linked to timber and lumber operations. They assumed that lumbermen, in removing the trees, helped to clear land that could then be turned into farms. The new farmers would not only be able to supply the lumber camps with food, but would add to their income by working as lumberjacks during the long winters when farm activities slowed down. Settlement had occurred in this way in Southern Ontario, and it was assumed that the process would be repeated in the north. In fact it was not repeated, largely because the soil and climate of Northern Ontario are very different from those farther south.

Coincidentally, however, the small pockets of agricultural settlement in Northern Ontario in the late 19th century were roughly the same areas as the white pine areas. These were along the north shore of Lake Huron, at the Lakehead, and in the Rainy River–Lake of the Woods district. The settlers in these areas owned their land, having acquired it from the provincial government by purchase or free grant. All of the other land and the forest on it was Crown property, which the lumbermen required permission to enter and cut.

Once the provincial government had made a survey the lumber operators sent in a few men, often local Indians who knew the area well, to make an estimate (or cruise) of the lumber. They then applied to the government for a licence to cut. This licence specified the size and exact location of the timber limit assigned to that operator, the amount to be cut each year, and the fees to be paid. Once given permission to cut, the operator sent his men (many of them Québecois, who by this time had become legendary lumberjacks) into the bush.

Until the 1940s bush operations in Northern Ontario were seasonal and heavily dependent on streams, rivers, and lakes to get the logs from the forest to the mill. Logs are bulky and heavy, and not very valuable in relation to their size and weight. Cheap transport was a necessity, and water transport was cheapest over long distances.

Like other skilled occupations, bush workers had their own specialties and technical language. The swampers, fellers, and sawyers went into the forest in September to cut tote roads and set up camp by building a large log bunkhouse or shanty in which they could all live for the next three to six months. Working throughout the fall from dawn to dusk with only axes and saws, they would hurl down the pine and saw it into logs eight to twenty feet long. These logs were then stacked into piles known as skidways or rollways. When the ground froze and the snow came, the skidders and haulers took over, carrying the logs by horsedrawn sleighs over man-made ice roads to the nearest river. When spring thaw opened up the river, the logs were floated or driven downstream to the sawmills, where circular, band, and gang saws cut them into boards and planks.

Each summer during the 1880s and '90s pine logs were driven in ever-larger numbers down the French, Spanish, and Mississagi rivers into storage booms on the north shore of Lake Huron. Some were destined for new sawmill towns such as Spragge, Blind River, and Thessalon. Many more were formed into huge rafts (some containing more than 50,000 logs and covering fifteen acres) and were towed to mills in Michigan, while others were loaded into schooners and shipped to ports as far away as Sarnia and Chicago. In the same years American lumbermen were cutting the forests at the western end of the province, treating them as extensions of the pineries of

4-8 *A lumber camp bunkhouse north of Capreol in the 1920s. The two-tiered, two-man berths were called muzzle-loaders, since the men crawled in, head first, with feet toward the fire. Unsanitary conditions in the bunkhouses were often a source of discontent.*

4-9 *Oscar Styffe established and operated Oscar Styffe Ltd. in Port Arthur, a company specializing in timber contracting and lake shipping. He served on Port Arthur council in 1935, and in 1941 was appointed Norwegian vice-consul for the area.*

4-10 *Children earned their keep, as did the dogs. While chopping and hauling firewood, these North Bay boys are learning skills that may later become a livelihood.*

4-8

4-9

4-10

4-11 *The camp kitchen at Hawk Depot, about 1940. Although the workers' lodgings often left much to be desired, there was always an abundance of good food.*

4-12 *Transporting supplies to camps on the Blind River, 1920s. The steam-powered Alligator tugs were invaluable freight carriers, since they could winch themselves over a portage.*

4-13 *The McFadden Lumber Co. camp at Lake Matinenda in the 1930s. The mill operations at Blind River, which were fed by camps such as these, began in 1853 with the Savail sawmill and continued until 1970.*

4-11

4-12

4-13

Wisconsin and Minnesota. In these early years, both on the north shore of Lake Huron and in the Rainy River–Lake of the Woods area, American needs and markets dictated the exploitation pattern of Northern Ontario's forests.

This pattern was soon changed by government policies. The federal government committed itself to promoting the construction of the Canadian Pacific Railway, and the Northern Ontario sections of this line were built between 1875 and 1885. The actual construction of the railway required large amounts of wood for ties, piles, bridge timbers, and stations. Previously ignored trees such as tamarack, cedar, and spruce were best suited for some of these purposes, so they began to be cut in large numbers. The railway also reduced, though it did not eliminate, lumbering's dependence on water transport. Sawmills and shipping points for logs and lumber sprouted up wherever the line crossed a driveable river. Most importantly, the railway opened up new markets for Northern Ontario forest products, especially on the prairies.

The trend to local milling was given a boost by the action of the Ontario government. In 1898 it prohibited the export from the province of sawlogs cut on Crown lands. Immediately some of the American lumbermen began to build sawmills in the Sudbury, Georgian Bay, Rainy River, and Kenora-Keewatin districts. Some of these mills continued to supply the American market, but with sawn lumber, not logs, because of the "manufacturing condition." Most also produced for the Canadian market, both east and west.

When the Canadian Northern Railway was built across Northern Ontario in the years before World War I, more areas of the forest were opened up and the shift to local milling for home markets increased. This was especially so in the Clay Belt, where prospects for agriculture and more intensive settlement seemed much better than elsewhere in Northern Ontario. Sawmills spread west from Cochrane along the new line. The railway was especially vital to the lumber industry in this area, because it lay north of the height-of-land; since the rivers

there flowed into Hudson Bay, they could not be used to supply southern markets.

By 1914 a new pattern had been established for lumbering in Northern Ontario. Agricultural settlement, though slow and very limited by prairie standards, offered a local market, food supplies, and a labour force for the industry. White pine, the most important tree in the past, rapidly disappeared before the axe and the saw. Spruce, jack pine, and balsam took its place, in some markets at least. Rivers were still used for transportation wherever possible, since they were the cheapest way to move logs, but railways offered an alternative, especially for sawn lumber.

While the amount of wood cut, sawn, and shipped grew for a time, competition from British Columbia eventually reduced Northern Ontario to a poor second in the national and international lumber business. Fortunately, a new force appeared on the scene: the pulp-and-paper industry. Although it reinforced some of the existing practices and tendencies of forest use, it changed many of the fundamental conditions of that use, and of life and work, in Northern Ontario. When it appeared, Northern Ontario's forests came into their own.

By the end of the 19th century the United States was running short of wood that was suitable for pulping and situated close enough to the large eastern cities. At the same time the American demand for newsprint was growing by leaps and bounds. Northern Ontario's forests had a high proportion of spruce, one of the very best woods for pulp and paper, and the region also had the large amounts of water needed for the industry. With incentives provided to American entrepreneurs by the Ontario government, Northern Ontario had largely switched to pulp-and-paper operations by the mid-1920s.

There are two significant differences between the operations of the pulp-and-paper mills and the lumber industry. Compared with the average sawmills, pulp-and-paper mills are bigger, more complex, and place a much heavier demand on the forest. They require large amounts of capital, more technically trained workers, a wood supply guaranteed over many years, and massive

4-14 *Cutting crews in the square-timber trade consisted of three men. A chopper notched the tree and determined precisely where it would fall. Two sawyers felled it with a cross-cut saw. The chopper then topped and limbed the tree, and the sawyers cut it into 10 or 12-foot lengths. These men probably worked in the Mississagi River area around 1910.*

4-15 *This skid of sawlogs is being hauled for the Pigeon River Lumber Co.'s mill at Port Arthur in the early 1900s. The younger members of the crew in the foreground did the lighter work at all levels of the lumbering operation.*

4-16 *A small log jam in the rapids near Blind River around 1910. This one could be cleared up by the men, but sometimes the jams had to be dynamited.*

amounts of water (for the pulping processes) and power (for the giant papermaking machines). Second, pulp mills can use trees of much smaller diameter than sawmills can, which meant that more trees in any given area were cut, and these were sawed into shorter lengths (normally 4-foot bolts). It was common to assign each cutter a strip from which he could cut all of the merchantable trees and stack the bolts in a 4'×4'×8' pile known as a cord. The cord remained the standard measure of pulpwood until very recently. One cord yielded approximately one ton of groundwood pulp, one ton of newsprint, or half a ton of chemical pulp.

More men went into the bush; some worked for mill companies, others for contractors. In 1929 Northern Ontario pulp-and-paper companies consumed approximately one million cords of wood, but with the onset of the Depression the bottom fell out of the vital American market. Production dropped drastically, a number of mills plagued by shaky finances went into receivership, and employment plummeted.

Some bitter strikes occurred, the more famous of them spearheaded by Finnish immigrants who, in addition to a radical approach to labour relations, also introduced new standards of cleanliness into the bush. Finnish-run camps were noted for the fact that they frequently were family operations, employed women as cooks and laundry workers, and usually built a sauna before anything else. Production and employment began to rise again in the late 1930s, and by World War II the labour situation became so tight that hundreds of German prisoners of war were used in bush operations.

The years since World War II have seen a new era in the history of Northern Ontario's forests—the era of forestry. It has been made necessary and possible by a revolution in the operations of lumber and pulp-and-paper companies—a revolution based on the internal-combustion engine. The same force that began to alter the lives of all North Americans in the 1920s entered the forests of Northern Ontario in the 1940s, and has since altered almost every aspect of life and work there.

Mechanization began in a small way with the introduction of the gasoline-powered chain saw. The early models were heavy and needed two men to operate them, but they were soon replaced by highly efficient (if still *very* noisy) lighter models. The amount of wood that could be cut by one man increased by roughly 25 percent almost overnight. Axes and handsaws disappeared. Horses for hauling wood in the bush disappeared equally quickly and were entirely gone by the mid-1960s, replaced by a combination bulldozer and small crane known as a wheeled skidder. At the same time, all-weather roads and large trucks marked the end of water transport as the cheapest way to bring logs to the mill. Soon the old methods were gone: skilled axemen were replaced by chainsaw operators, teamsters and river drivers by mechanics and truck drivers. Logging no longer depended on the seasons, and year-round bush operations became normal.

The roads built to get the logs out also allowed many loggers to commute to work, or at least to get to the nearest town every weekend, instead of spending months in remote bush camps. The camps took on a completely new appearance, with prefabricated and heated garages and repair shops, separate rooms for every two or three men, laundry facilities, showers, games rooms, and modern cafeterias. Only in this last instance did things remain the same as before—lumber camps kept their reputation for more than adequate amounts of good, solid, food!

The changes are still going on, with the latest developments in the forests focusing on the introduction of mechanical tree harvesters, which can reduce an entire growing tree to pulpwood in less than a minute. In the mills lumber, pulp and paper, plywood, and many other products are now commonly manufactured on the same site, and research into improved production methods and new ways of utilizing wood has become a standard part of industry operations.

Today's forest-product companies consume far larger amounts of wood than would earlier have been dreamed possible. It is here that forestry enters the picture. Forestry may be defined as "the scientific management of forests so as to produce continuous crops of trees." Until very recently forestry has been the sole responsibility of the provincial government. It has leased, not sold, Crown

4–14

4–15

4–16

4-17

4-18

4-17 *These men and horses worked at a sawmill in the Rainy River area, likely Devlin or La Vallee, around 1910. This is a typical mill, with its wood pile, tote wagons, a boiler, and a covered saw shed, which housed a stationary circular saw.*

4-18 *A new boiler being installed at the Shevlin-Clarke sawmill, Fort Frances, about 1910.*

lands to private individuals or companies. The government acts as landlord, and the lumber and pulp-and-paper companies act as tenants who purchase licences to cut the timber. Like any landlord, the government has tried to find tenants who pay the rent regularly and provide employment in forest-based industries. Until recently there has been less concern with conserving resources and more with encouraging their profitable use, because in the past stumpage dues and ground rents have been a major source of government income. Even if forestry had been a priority, there were few professionally trained foresters and little scientific knowledge of the complex life systems that make up a forest. The first school of forestry in Canada was established at the University of Toronto only in 1907.

For all these reasons forestry played only a small role in Northern Ontario until after World War II. There were some signs of interest before then; beginning in 1907, the government set aside approximately 12,000 square miles of forest reserves in the Temagami, Mississagi, Nipigon, and Quetico areas, but these were not managed in any systematic manner. Tree planting on a very small scale began in the 1920s around Kirkwood. The same decade saw the first comprehensive survey of all the province's forest resources, but the Depression prevented any follow-up. The first clear signs of forestry on a large scale in Northern Ontario came in the area of fire protection.

Fire is one of the most destructive agents in the forest, and it is certainly one of the most spectacular. As more settlers, railway workers, and miners entered the north, the likelihood of fire grew and the dangers became apparent: 1910, Rainy River, 300 square miles burned, 42 dead; 1911, Porcupine, 800 square miles burned, 73 dead; 1916, Matheson, 1,000 square miles burned, 223 dead. Public attention coincided with technical innovation in this area. In the 1920s lookout towers were erected, telephone (and later radio) links were installed, and government aircraft based in Sault Ste. Marie were used as flying observation posts and in emergency evacuations.

Only in the 1950s and '60s and after a major reorganization of the Department of Lands and Forests (now the Ministry of Natural Resources) did forestry really begin in Northern Ontario, as a number of developments converged. The mechanization of cutting operations, the increasing distances over which wood had to be trucked to the mills, the need to modernize mills to meet threats of competition from the West Coast and the southern United States, and the new uses to which wood and paper were being put all led the forest industries to question where future wood supplies might come from and to employ trained foresters in growing numbers. Foresters began to gain experience in working for both government and industry, and to see the need for closer co-operation between the two.

Scientific knowledge of the region's forests reached a point where it could move out of the laboratory and into the bush, and the province established a second school of forestry, now part of Lakehead University. Public interest in the forest also grew rapidly, partly because of increased leisure time and the resulting demand for recreational facilities, and partly because of the growing environmental movement. These developments emphasized a new problem in the forests—the concept of multiple use, and the question of how to put it into practice. Recently forest inventories and attempts to draw up strategic land-use plans have produced heated debates among public and private foresters, hunters, fishermen, campers, Indian bands, wildlife biologists, and wilderness enthusiasts. Even while these debates were going on, the massive fires of 1980 were a reminder that man is still very far from being able to control nature at will.

Nevertheless the future of lumbering, pulp and paper, and forestry in the region depends on the systematic management of the forests and upon co-operative action by all forest users. The eras of white pine and white spruce, which gave little thought to future supplies, have given way to the era of forestry, still in its infancy. The intensive exploitation of the forests of Northern Ontario has occurred only in the past one hundred years. Careful forest-management practices by all users will ensure a strong and vital industry for years to come.

4-19 *A 1940 view of the sawing operation at a Rainy Lake sawmill.*

4-20 *The interior of an engine room at the Austin Nicholson Lumber Co. The boy at the right may have been an errand boy and grease monkey. The safety conditions are far from ideal; clothing caught on the drive belts could pull a worker to his death or amputate a limb.*

4-21 *A lumber yard in the Rainy River district, 1920s. Green lumber is being stacked in piles to dry; later it will be loaded onto freight cars for transportation to markets.*

4-19

4-20

4-21

4-22 *This E.B. Eddy employee on the Spanish River near Espanola is wearing mosquito or black fly netting so that he can concentrate on his work.*

4-24 *River drivers portaging a pointer on the Mississagi River, 1949.*

4-23 *When the ice melted, booms of sawlogs and pulpwood were towed across lakes by straining oarsmen in small boats called pointers. This pointer is carrying a crew of sweepers on the Mississagi River in 1949.*

4-22

4-23

4-24

4-25 *A Wakami Lumber Co. worker at Sultan, 1948.*

4-26 *Two Finnish pulpcutters in the Nipigon area, mid-1920s. By 1920 most of the woodcutters were recent European immigrants and seasonal workers from Quebec. The cutting gang was being phased out in favour of the pieceworker, who went into the bush alone with his buck saw.*

4-27 *A card game with musical entertainment at the Kormac camp in 1949. The camp mascot occupies the centre of the table.*

4-28 *When the saw logs arrived at the mill site, they were sorted at a jack ladder, which lifted the logs up into the mill. This crew worked at the lower end of the Mississagi River in 1947.*

4-25

4-26

4-27

4-28

4–29 *Women pour coffee for strikers at Timmins, 1946.*

4–30 *A woodsman using a power chainsaw at Camp 60, Ontario Paper Co., Manitouwadge, White River, 1957.*

4–31 *In the new mill operations, the machine shop replaced the blacksmith's shop. This machinist worked at the Sheppard and Morse lumber camp near Chapleau in 1949.*

4–32 *A Drott skid-loader loads a truck near Thunder Bay. The efficiency of these front-end loaders doomed horse power in the logging industry.*

4–33 *A Linn tractor hauling Wakami Lumber Co. logs over a snow road near Sultan in the late 1940s.*

4–29

4–30

4–31

4–32

4–33

4-34 *Loading pulpwood onto a freighter at Port Arthur, 1951. The pulp logs are much smaller than the logs required for lumber.*

4-35 *A tree harvester at work near Ignace in 1969. This Great Lakes Paper Co. harvester cuts the trees and loads the logs with its grappling arm.*

4-36 *With increased harvesting efficiency and year-round cutting operations, the depletion of the forests is a very real possibility. The nurturing of the forests is now an important aspect of the industry. Carol Mackenzie, Ministry of Natural Resources Forester at Thunder Bay and Kenora, tends new growth in 1980.*

4-34

4-35

4-36

CHAPTER FIVE

ANGUS GILBERT
Associate Professor of History and Dean of Social Sciences,
Laurentian University,
Sudbury.

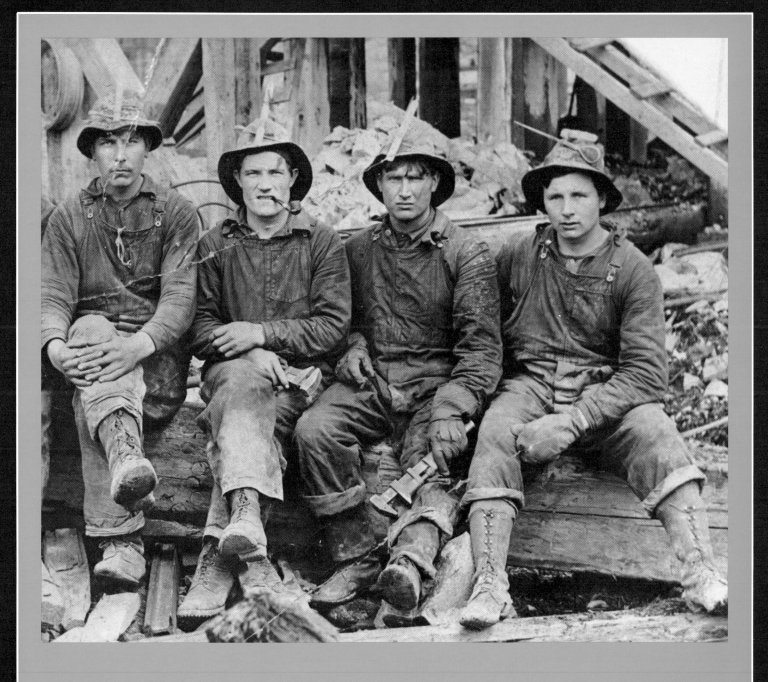

5-1 *At the Creighton Mine, 1907. These men*
are dressed like other labourers of the time—
cotton clothing, rubber and leather boots, and
soft hats—but with candles.

5–2 *A Timmins prospector and his home, about 1912.*

5–3 *Gradually mining communities developed that offered more comfort than the prospector's tent. These are the miners' homes at the Silver Mountain Mine in 1899, being inspected by members of the legislative tour of that year.*

5–4 *The best-known names in Northern Ontario are those of prospectors who founded producing mines. In 1909 Alex Gillies (left) and Benny Hollinger staked the Hollinger Mine property near what later became Timmins. The Hollinger Mine eventually had 360 miles of tunnels. It closed in 1968, after 58 years of gold production that totalled over $566 million.*

5–5 *A gold assay shop in Timmins, manned by Harry H. Miller and Tommy Huff.*

5–2

5–3

5–4

5–5

5-6

5-7

Ontario's landscape is dominated by the Canadian Shield. Two-thirds of the province and nearly all of the north is covered by a mosaic of rock, lake, and forest created by the caprice of geological history. Hundreds of millions of years before there was any animal life on earth, molten rock welled up from deep within the earth toward its surface, carrying with it metals and minerals that remained after the rock had cooled and solidified. The features of the northern landscape were then rearranged by great glaciers creeping south, scraping and scouring everything in their path. They moved masses of rock and soil, creating new lakes and rivers that changed the drainage patterns, exposed mineral deposits in some places, and buried them deep under debris in others. It was a double-edged legacy: the shield held minerals of tremendous variety and value; at the same time the sheer wildness and brutality of the landscape defied men to find and exploit them.

The minerals of the Canadian Shield are now an essential part of the Ontario economy. It was not always so. For much of the 19th century the shield was seen, not as a mineral-rich territory waiting to be exploited, but as a useless barrier blocking the northern and western expansion of agricultural settlement. In 1864 the Toronto *Globe* dismissed it as "gaps of rough and…barren country which lie between us and the fertile prairies of North-western British America." A market could always be found for the timber, but of what conceivable use were rocks?

This failure to grasp the significance of the wealth that lay within the shield is hardly surprising. Mining in the north could only be difficult. Obviously markets, capital, and labour were necessary, but even more important were technology and cheap transportation to permit exploration, to bring men and supplies in, and to ship ore out. The pattern was there from the beginning and it was inescapable: mines would be developed by and for outsiders. Circumstances also dictated another pattern, at least in the beginning: mining development would depend on the building of railways, but since railways were built for other purposes, mineral discoveries would be made haphazardly and by chance, despite the work of the Geological Survey of Canada begun in 1843.

The two exceptions to this pattern, Bruce Mines and Silver Islet, both owned by the Montreal Mining Company, merely emphasize this. The earliest mines of any significance in Northern Ontario, they could be reached by water and as a result were easily developed. Copper deposits at Bruce Mines, about thirty-five miles east of Sault Ste. Marie, were purchased by the company in 1846. Mining began a few years later and continued fitfully for a quarter of a century. At its height the mine employed 350 men and boys, 200 of whom worked underground. The project seemed plagued by bad luck. The first enginehouse collapsed in 1848 when the machinery was first started up. A few years later an attempt to smelt ore near the mine ended when the smelter burned to the ground. In 1862 the village was destroyed by a bush fire. The ore was not handled efficiently; transportation costs,

5-12 *Underground at the Evans Mine, Copper Cliff, 1890. Soft hats offer little protection and candles provide little light for these miners.*

5-13 *The Helen Mine, near present-day Wawa, was named after F. H. Clergue's sister. First discovered by Ben Boyer in 1898, it was bought by Clergue to supply his steel mills and mined from 1900 to 1918. In 1939 it was reopened and used as an open-pit mine until 1950.*

5-14 *The cookhouse at the Casey Mine near New Liskeard in 1904. In this case it seems to be the man who is the cook.*

5-12

5-13

5-14

pushing the Temiskaming and Northern Ontario Railway (T & NO) north from North Bay. The railway was designed to provide a new agricultural frontier for Ontario in the clay belts. The discovery of the mineral was, as in Sudbury, purely accidental, but Cobalt was unlike Sudbury in another respect: it was, at first, a poor man's camp. Whatever the truth of the legend that Fred LaRose, a blacksmith with the T & NO, uncovered a vein of silver when he threw his hammer at a fox, it is true that at Cobalt it was possible to extract high-grade silver ore with equipment no more sophisticated than a pick and shovel. Small wonder that hordes of would-be prospectors flocked to the area.

There was one incorporated mining company in Cobalt in 1903; by 1907 there were five hundred in the area. But only twenty-nine mines were operating, which gives some indication of the wild speculation going on. Cobalt very early developed the reputation of a wide-open mining town—which it was. But the darker side of life in these early mining camps was reflected in the miners' strike of 1907 against the Cobalt mine owners and in the accident statistics indicating that in 1910, for example, underground fatalities at Cobalt were 12 per 1,000.

Cobalt kept its mystique for a long time, but mining there soon became an expensive business. Once the rich outcrops were exhausted, more exploration was necessary. In 1909 seventeen drills were at work. Open-pit mining was replaced by shafts. Lower-grade ores were used, ores that needed processing before being shipped out. Wood, coal, and an ingenious experiment to pump compressed air through miles of pipeline eventually gave way to electricity to power the mills.

Silver production at Cobalt peaked in 1911, but the Cobalt experience had already made its mark on mining development. Cobalt was the mother camp for Elk Lake and Gowganda, for Porcupine and Kirkland Lake. Prospectors are restless souls, always searching for a new frontier, but rarely do they have the resources to exploit the finds they make. As mining became more difficult and capital-intensive at Cobalt, the mines consolidated and the weaker operators were forced out. Cobalt exported

experience and men and provided the capital to finance further exploration and development.

The Timmins brothers, Noah and Henry, were examples of this connection. Starting as Mattawa merchants, they shrewdly put up the capital to finance the development of the Cobalt deposit discovered by Fred LaRose. Their profits from LaRose's mine helped them to develop the Hollinger Mine at Porcupine. This unusual availability of capital allowed prospectors to explore areas not directly served by the railway. The rush to Elk Lake and Gowganda began in 1907; by 1909 close to one thousand teams of horses were hauling freight to and from Gowganda. The costs were enormous, but not high enough to dampen enthusiasm.

By 1910 the Gowganda silver mines were sending out ore, but they were soon overshadowed by the discovery of major gold deposits at Porcupine, even further from the railway. Transportation wasn't the only problem at Porcupine; its ore required an expensive chemical-separation process to free the gold. Because of the difficulties and cost of transporting low-grade ores, the mineral had to be processed on the spot. This required power, and electricity was not available at Timmins until the mid-1920s. What all of this meant was that development of the Porcupine fields could only be undertaken by men who commanded large amounts of capital. This was certainly no poor man's camp.

Gold was first discovered in 1909 in Whitney and Tisdale townships. Again the first strike was made by accident. A prospector slipped on a rock, stripping off the moss and exposing stringers of gold. Benny Hollinger staked the Hollinger Mine, J.S. Wilson the Dome, and Sandy McIntyre the McIntyre. All three were prospectors who had been grubstaked by wealthier patrons. Certainly none of them was in any position to develop his find. Sandy McIntyre, for example, had fled to Canada to escape a nagging wife (or so he said). Born Alexander Oliphant in Scotland, he changed his name and his country, found work with the T & NO construction gangs, and took to prospecting, which became his second love. Unfortunately his first was the bottle, which may explain his sale of his Porcupine claims for a pittance. His claims produced millions in gold, but McIntyre received very little of it. It was investors such as the Timmins brothers, who had made their fortunes at Cobalt, who were in a position to develop Porcupine.

By 1912 the railway had made its way to South Porcupine and Timmins, but development was temporarily delayed by the disastrous bush fires of 1911. In May the Hollinger Mine lost its surface plant and buildings. Worse was to come. On July 11 most of the surface plants and the town of South Porcupine were destroyed. Over seventy people lost their lives, many as a result of fleeing to the mine shafts, where they suffocated as the oxygen was sucked out by the fires raging above. Despite these setbacks Timmins and South Porcupine were there to stay.

Hard on the heels of the Porcupine finds came the discovery of gold at Kirkland Lake in 1911 by W.H. Wright and in 1912 by the Tough brothers and Harry Oakes. Development here was a little easier. Although a T & NO branch did not reach Kirkland Lake until 1923, the road connection to the railway was much shorter and easier than it was for Timmins-Porcupine. The ore bodies were richer as well. This easier development accounted for Harry Oakes's almost unique success story. Oakes, a penniless prospector, through sheer tenacity developed his claims into his own mine, the Lake Shore, the greatest of the early Kirkland Lake mines. Unfortunately his unpleasant personality, together with the mystery surrounding his murder, have obscured his achievement.

The Porcupine and Kirkland Lake discoveries marked the end of the era of free-wheeling, hit-and-miss lucky strikes. Ontario had now become the leading mining province by far, accounting for over 40 percent of total Canadian production by 1914 and employing 11,000 workers in mining in Northern Ontario. World War I created an even greater market for minerals, but it also dried up the investment capital needed for further exploration and development. After the war things were never quite the same, as the bush plane suddenly freed prospectors from the tether of the railways. Mining development still required railways, but the exploration phase was now

independent, and in future the location of railway lines would often be determined by the location of mines. The master-servant relationship was reversed.

Two developments marked the period between the wars: existing mining properties were consolidated in the northeast, and new gold fields were explored in the northwest. At Sudbury the International Nickel Company merged with the Mond Nickel Company, but this did not create a monopoly: Falconbridge Nickel Mines had been created in 1928. Production increased in the northeastern gold mines by leaps and bounds as mining properties were consolidated. In 1939 the Kerr-Addison Mine was created by amalgamating several properties at Larder Lake, which finally began producing in a big way. As the silver mines declined, however, the mining population had to shift from town to town.

Since no significant new finds were made in Northeastern Ontario, the Cobalt–Porcupine–Kirkland Lake frontier turned east and west after the war. In the east it moved out of the province into Quebec, but it was in the northwest that Ontario found a new bonanza. As early as 1894 the Geological Survey of Canada had suggested that gold could be found at Red Lake. A few early claims had been staked, but Red Lake's remoteness had stymied development. Finally in 1925 two parties led by the Howey brothers, Lorne and Ray—one grubstaked by Haileybury businessmen and the other employed by McIntyre Porcupine Mines—simultaneously discovered gold at Red Lake. They unleashed what became probably the biggest rush since the Klondike. The rush resembled the Klondike in another way: dog teams, for the last time in Ontario, played a major role in transporting goods to and from Red Lake. They were gradually replaced by bush planes, which soon proved their usefulness in prospecting as well, for example, in the 1928 gold discovery at Pickle Lake.

Meanwhile another important find was made in the northwest, this one following earlier patterns of exploration. In the heyday of transcontinental railway building before World War I the Canadian Northern had pushed another line across Northern Ontario, north of the CPR

5–15

5–16

5-17 *Captain Albert Johnson supervised the mines employment office in Cobalt in 1910.*

5-18 *Workers posing among Cobalt's silver production in the 1910s. By 1907 Cobalt produced 10 million ounces, and in 1911 Canada's silver production peaked at 31 million ounces, making it the world's third-largest producer.*

5-17

5-18

line. During the war the surveys of the Ontario Department of Mines and the Geological Survey of Canada found traces of gold along the Canadian Northern line between Lake Nipigon and Long Lac. Prospectors, who had come to rely on these surveys, began working the area in the 1920s, at first making only small finds. In 1931 the search culminated in the discovery of a major gold field at Little Long Lac by "Hard Rock" Bill Smith, a veteran of the Porcupine and Red Lake rushes.

The other major discovery of the interwar period was the massive iron deposit at Steep Rock Lake, 140 miles west of Thunder Bay. Since the closing of the Helen Mine at Michipicoten in 1918, no iron ore had been mined in Canada. It took six years to bring Steep Rock into production. Earlier development costs were as nothing compared with the money needed here to mine an ore body at the bottom of a seven-square-mile lake. Eventually the lake, 100 billion gallons of it, was drained and a river was diverted before open-pit mining could begin.

Canadian industrial growth during World War II gave a great boost to mining, especially in the base-metal sector. This time the demand did not fall at the end of the war, and through the 1950s and '60s production of most minerals remained high, after doubling in Ontario between 1945 and 1951. This production came mainly from long-established mines, including a renewed working of Cobalt's deposits in 1949. There were some exceptions, the most notable resulting from the discovery of uranium between Sudbury and Sault Ste. Marie in 1955. Elliot Lake emerged almost overnight, as production skyrocketed from $9.4 million in 1956 to $24.62 million in 1959, and employment climbed from 1,462 to 9,633. Ominously, production dropped back to $38.8 million within a decade, and Elliot Lake appeared to be dying until a dramatic improvement began in the 1970s.

From 1959 to 1969, when uranium markets seemed to be disappearing, the gold mines were also in trouble. Employment dropped by 50 percent, much of it in Timmins and Kirkland Lake, although the discovery of a massive zinc-copper deposit near Timmins in 1964 softened the blow. The result included the Kidd Creek Mine

and larger smelters. To the west a copper and base-metals deposit discovered at Manitouwadge in 1957 was also exploited. Several small iron mines were also opened or reopened at this time at Temagami (Dofasco), Capreol (National Steel), Kirkland Lake (Jones and Laughlin), Wawa (Algoma Steel), Red Lake, and Bruce Lake. A number of these have since been closed, which is not an encouraging sign. On the other hand, the rise in the price of gold in the late 1970s stimulated a resurgence of exploration and led to two promising new discoveries: one at Detour Lake, north of Timmins, and the other at Hemlo, east of Marathon. In the 1970s the shores of Sturgeon Lake, northeast of Ignace, became the site of several zinc-copper-lead mines.

By the late 1970s, however, the future of the mining industry in general seemed less hopeful. This had worrisome implications for all those Northern Ontario communities that depended on the mines for their livelihood. A long period of prosperity and expansion had obscured the structural weaknesses in the system, weaknesses that could not be eliminated by the exploration and development of new mineral deposits. A century of development had created a sparse and scattered population across the shield. Despite their best efforts, most communities were almost entirely dependent on the extraction and processing of a single resource. They were subject to crucial decisions made in distant corporate offices that were insulated from the devastating local impact of these decisions. Dependence on outside investment capital made this inevitable, but the recognition of this fact does not lower the level of frustration. Mining has been dependent on external markets in the United States, Western Europe, and Japan, and this too has meant reliance on forces over which Northern Ontario has no control. This has been aggravated by recent market competition in the mining sector, especially from Third World countries.

The mining industry has tried to respond to these pressures by diversifying and by increasing productivity. Diversification has usually taken the form of recovering what had been regarded as secondary minerals. This diversification has made the mining communities somewhat less vulnerable, but now the thrust toward increased productivity poses a new threat. The industry is now relying more and more on technology and mechanization, and increased production is possible even with decreasing levels of employment. The most striking example of this is at Sudbury, where the International Nickel Company's work force has shrunk from over 20,000 to less than half that number.

Mining has been a mixed blessing for Northern Ontario. It has provided wealth and promoted settlement. At the same time it has helped to create and perpetuate the north's role as a hinterland for the south, eternally at the mercy of external forces.

5-19

5-20

5-21 *Schumacher townsite and the McIntyre Mine, 1912. Schumacher was originally called Aura Lake, but was renamed for Frederick Schumacher, an Ohio druggist who bought and sold property on the townsite. In his will he left $1,000 annually to provide Christmas presents for local schoolchildren.*

5-22 *Sandy McIntyre, the Scottish iron moulder whose claims became the McIntyre Porcupine gold mine. He made little money from the sale of his claims and was saved from poverty by a company pension.*

5-23 *Mining syndicates were important in the financing and development of mining operations. A sleigh caboose housed the Howey Red Lake Gold Syndicate's office in Hudson in 1926.*

5-21

5-22

5-23

5-24 *Unions attempted to improve working conditions as well as the workers' share of the profits. This 1913 parade of Timmins and South Porcupine strikers includes many immigrant workers who had brought radical labour traditions with them to Canada.*

5-25 *In the engine house at the Creighton Mine. The men who ran the hoist held their co-workers' lives at the end of a steel cable.*

5-24

5-25

5-26 *Underground beside the cage in the Porcupine, about 1920.*

5-27 *Drilling in the mines, Cobalt, about 1900.*

5-28 *Falconbridge miners loading ore or "muck" into a car at the bottom of a chute, 1940s. By this time, hardhat lights were common.*

5–26

5-27

5–28

5-29 *George Campbell (left) discovered one of the western world's richest gold mines —Campbell Red Lake. Here, at his home (Hell's Acres) in 1943, he charts a flight with Harold Farrington, one of the first pilots at Red Lake. Campbell occasionally hired Farrington to fly him to Toronto for a drink.*

5-30 *The largest gold producer in the Geraldton area was the McLeod Mosher Mine, which operated from 1938 to 1970. Here that mine's second gold brick is being poured.*

5-31 *This mine-rescue team worked in Geraldton in the 1950s. Gold was discovered in the Geraldton-Beardmore area during the 1930s. Today, gold-mining development centres on Hemlo to the south, near Marathon.*

5-32 *After many years of sometimes violent struggle, labour and management must still attempt to negotiate conflicting interests. This is a labour-management production committee meeting at the Timmins Hollinger Mine in 1953.*

5-33 *Attempts to organize union locals in Sudbury-area mines were made as early as 1912, but only during World War II were*

5-29

5-30

5-31

5-32

5-33

they finally successful. Reid Robinson, president of the Mine, Mill and Smelter Workers, addressed Local 598 members and their families in 1943.

5-34 A dredge in the Steep Rock Lake-Atikokan area, 1955. As early as 1897, hematite boulders on the shores of Steep Rock Lake indicated a substantial ore body under the water.

5-35 As new technology developed, miners' work shifted from hacking and hauling to heavy-equipment operation. Here a mucking machine does the mucking-out at Falconbridge's Fraser Mine, Onaping area, in 1981.

5-36 The open-pit iron mine at Steep Rock Lake, 1967.

5-34

5-35

5-36

5-37 *The Hollinger Mine in the 1950s. The work areas and recreation areas became integrated; beside the old headframe is a new refining mill, power plant, and baseball diamond.*

5-38 *Creighton No. 3 shaft and town in the early 1930s. As families moved into the developing mining communities, companies began to design and build towns for them. This photo shows some evidence of town planning.*

5-37

5-38

CHAPTER SIX Agriculture and Settlement

ROMAN BROZOWSKI
Associate Professor of Geography and Dean of Arts,
Nipissing University College,
North Bay.

KEITH TOPPS
Associate Professor of Geography,
Nipissing University College,
North Bay.

DAVID REES
Associate Professor of Geography,
Nipissing University College,
North Bay.

6–1 *Farm-lot timber was usually the settler's first*
cash crop. As the land was cleared, the
timber was cut and sold to the nearest lumber
company. This 1919 New Liskeard-area
farm family lived near enough to a mill to
build their house and barn from boards and
planks. The smaller outbuildings were
probably of pole or log construction. The
bush lot remains an important source of
building materials and fuel for farmers.

6-2

6-3

6–2 When the timber was removed, the stump land was burned over. Although this was easier than digging up the stumps, burning destroyed the topsoil and its nutrients. In some areas the soil was so thin that the "slash and burn" technique made it unsuitable for any agricultural purpose. This photograph was taken near Cochrane, around 1910.

6–3 The settler's first concern was for shelter and food. The land's timber provided the building materials for the house, and a small kitchen garden was begun. This small log home, with a rear kitchen made of lumber, was built in Fort Frances at the turn of the century.

6–4 This La Vallee-area farmer posed with the most important things on his farm: his wife and family, his draft animals, and his breeding stock. All were necessary to the

farm's success. The horse held by the man was probably the family "driver," used to pull vehicles.

6–5 After the timber had been cleared, the stones were culled from the fields. The potato field in the foreground yielded the pile of stones in front of the drive shed. This is a 1906 view of the Tucker farm, one of the first in Harris Township when it was established in 1895.

6–4

6–5

6–6 *Around the turn of the century, agriculture moved away from grain farming and toward dairy and livestock farming. The look of the farm changed, as small pen barns gave way to large timber-frame mow and stable barns. A skilled tradesman cut the beams and morticed the joints. Then, the neighbours and the farmer's extended family joined in the construction. Events like this barnraising in Emo helped to foster a sense of community.*

6–7 *Despite isolation, temperature extremes, insects, and a lack of government preparedness, many settlers persisted. This Kenora-district farmer found oxen, although they were slow, more sure-footed on the rough terrain than draft horses were. The single mouldboard plow was sometimes made by the local smith, but most were obtained from southern implement manufacturers.*

6–6

6–7

GEOGRAPHY AND CLIMATE have restricted farming in Northern Ontario to those regions that combine suitable soil conditions with an adequate growing season. These include the Little Clay Belt, running northward from Haileybury; the Great Clay Belt, stretching from Matheson to Hearst; the Nipissing low-lands; the Sudbury Basin; Manitoulin Island and the north shore of Lake Huron, especially in the vicinity of Sault Ste. Marie; the Thunder Bay district; and the Dryden, Kenora, Fort Frances, and Rainy River areas.

The history of agriculture has been closely tied to the other major economic activities in the north. Farming began as an offshoot of fur trading in the early 19th century and expanded with the appearance of lumbering and mining in the second half of the century. Most important, however, was the spreading network of railways, beginning with the Canadian Pacific in the 1880s and followed by the Temiskaming and Northern Ontario, the Canadian Northern, and the National Transcontinental in the 20th century, which opened up previously inaccessible arable lands.

Trading-post agriculture probably began with the first French and British traders in Northern Ontario. Certainly by the end of the 18th century it was commonplace. In the first two decades of the 19th century the most important agricultural settlement was at Fort William, the main supply depot for the entire North West Company fur trade. Both North West and Hudson's Bay personnel also kept herds of cattle and smaller livestock, and grew grain, potatoes, and other vegetables at such places as Fort Temiskaming, Sault Ste. Marie, Fort Frances, Brunswick House, and Ground Hog Lake. They still do so today at Moose Factory and Fort Albany.

As the lumbering industry began to move into the north in the mid-19th century, ready-made markets for agricultural goods were provided. Oats, hay, and pota-toes were required by the loggers and their horses, and because transportation costs from outside were so high, a good profit could be made by local production. Before the arrival of the railway, importing large numbers of cattle, sheep, and hogs was impractical, so the basic source of meat was from the hunt. Some farmers worked in the bush or hunted for wild game during the winter to supplement their income from farming in the summertime.

In the 1850s and '60s agricultural settlement followed lumbering out of the Ottawa-Mattawa valleys into the Little Clay Belt north of Lake Timiskaming and into the Lake Nipissing area. Many of the settlers came from Quebec; such French Canadian colonization and settlement brought to Northeastern Ontario the bilingual character that sets it apart from the rest of the province.

On Manitoulin Island, both lumbering and township surveys were begun in 1863, the first year that lands were opened to non-Indian occupation. The removal of the pine timber gradually cleared the way for agriculture. By 1871 over 300 of the island's approximately 2,000 people were farmers, mostly Ontario-born of British origin, from nearby Southern Ontario counties. They grew the crops they had grown before, such as barley, oats, vegetables, and hay for their sheep and cattle.

Elsewhere on the north shore of Lake Huron in the 1860s, lumbering, mineral discoveries at Bruce Mines, and the development of Sault Ste. Marie as a transportation centre encouraged agricultural settlement. By 1871 over 18,000 acres of land in the area were being farmed. In the Thunder Bay area, as the fur trade declined Fort William took on a new role as the busiest transshipment point on Lake Superior. Its growing population spurred the expansion of farming along the Kaministikwia River, and the mining activities on Silver Islet that began in the late 1860s provided new markets for the produce.

In the 1870s agriculture in Northern Ontario began to develop in a systematic fashion. This was largely because of the policies adopted by the provincial governments of John Sandfield Macdonald (1867-71) and Oliver Mowat (1871-96). By 1870 the best lands in Southern Ontario had been occupied, and farmers began to look to new frontiers in the American midwest and the Canadian northwest. In order to stem the tide of emigrants from the province, these governments portrayed Northern Ontario as a land of opportunity for farmers and passed a number of measures to encourage settlement.

The legislation that laid the basis for the agricultural development of the north was the Free Grants and Homestead Act of 1868, which opened to settlement selected free lands in the Nipissing and Algoma territories. Once surveyed, townships designated as free lands were made available to settlers on the basis of up to two hundred acres per head of household. For each child in the family over eighteen years of age, one hundred free acres were allowed. Provision was also made for settlers to buy additional land at a minimal price if they chose. Attached to the grants were conditions of clearing, cultivating, building construction, and a six-month-per-year residency requirement. Failure to meet these conditions ceded the land back to the Crown, and it became available to another settler.

Federal government policies also encouraged agricultural settlement in the 1870s, particularly in Northwestern Ontario. When Canada acquired Rupert's Land from the Hudson's Bay Company in 1870 the federal government built a road-and-water route linking Fort William to Fort Garry at the Red River. The Dawson Trail, as it became known, passed through potential farmland in the Rainy River area, opening it to lumbering. In 1873, with the signing of Indian Treaty No. 3, which ceded Ojibwa lands to the west of Lake Superior to the Dominion government, settlers began to flow into the region. By the late 1870s logs were being cut on both the American and Canadian sides of the border and taken by steamer to Fort Frances.

Farms established along the banks of the Rainy River depended largely on the lumber camps for markets, and as in Northeastern Ontario, farmers engaged in logging during the winter months. Fort William and Port Arthur also benefited from these polices; by 1881 about fifty-five farmers occupied over 1,500 acres of land near these communities. Oats and hay were grown for animal feed, and potatoes, turnips, and rye were the most important crops.

In Northeastern Ontario, Manitoulin Island and the North Channel area of Lake Huron led in terms of agricultural development in the 1870s. Here too, agriculture followed the spread of lumbering. Between 1871 and 1881, for example, there was an eightfold increase in the number of acres under cultivation along the north shore, and the number of farmers had increased to approximately nine hundred.

The lumbering industry along the Mattawa River also grew dramatically during that decade. Much of this growth occurred at Mattawa, but the other key centre was Nipissing Village, near the mouth of the South River on Lake Nipissing's south shore. The first citizen of Nipissing Village was a farmer, John Beatty, who came to the area via Mattawa in 1865. Until 1874 he remained isolated, but then a colonization road was constructed from Rosseau to a point near his farm. Nipissing Town-

6-8 *Many farms had two gardens. The kitchen garden, after it was ploughed and planted, was the woman's responsibility. The larger field gardens of potatoes, turnips, and subsistence vegetables were customarily prepared by the men and maintained by the whole family. Andrew Shuparski tends a garden in the Levack area.*

6-9 *In 1899, members of the Ontario legislature toured the northern part of the province to witness its development firsthand. Piper's farm in the Slate River Valley, Thunder Bay district, was a showpiece. The two-gabled house (behind the trees) indicates a prosperous operation.*

6-10 *The settlers who moved north continued to practise the farming methods they had used in the south—with varying degrees of success. Most planted wheat, which grew well in the humus of the arboreal forest but quickly depleted the rich yet thin soil. The grain cradle used by these Manitoulin Island farmers held the cut stalks gently, so as not to lose the grain heads. After cutting, the grain would be hand bound, stooked, and threshed.*

6-8

6-9

6-10

6-11

6-12

6-13

ship was surveyed, and agricultural settlement began in earnest. Within a decade, Nipissing Village's population had grown from nine families to over three hundred people.

The 1880s belonged to the railways, and as they made their way across the north, new towns sprang up, wagon trails were built to connect with the rail lines, and the population grew. The railways brought in not only settlers, but also seed, consumer goods, and above all, livestock. A mixed-farming economy began to develop.

In the Nipissing-to-Mattawa corridor, the population reached twelve thousand by 1891. From its inception in 1882, North Bay developed as a major transportation and commercial centre requiring a diversified local agricultural base. Other enduring new communities spawned by the railways—Powassan, Bonfield, Rutherglen, Verner, and Warren—served not only as lumbering and railway construction points, but became important farming centres.

Sudbury, a Canadian Pacific Railway (CPR) construction camp, was established on the northern shore of Lake Ramsey in 1883. Loggers and lumbermen soon arrived, and the agricultural lands in the "Basin" north of Sudbury, as well as the lands east and west of the village, were discovered. Chelmsford, Azilda, and Larchwood, communities that serviced both lumbering and agriculture, came into being. In the later 1880s mining provided additional local markets for settlers. By 1891 over one hundred farmers occupied more than 21,000 acres of land in the region, although of these only a few acres were under cultivation. The extension of the CPR branch line from Sudbury to Sault Ste. Marie in 1887 tied the North Channel settlements together and permitted year-round communications with other parts of the province. As a result, the number of farmers doubled in the decade, reaching 2,100 by 1891.

The impact of the CPR on agricultural development in Northwestern Ontario was equally dramatic. Rat Portage and Keewatin were transformed by the lumber industry, and the village became a central stopover for the several lake steamers that transported passengers, freight,

and lumber around the Lake of the Woods. By 1891 at least sixty-five farmers had taken up more than 9,000 acres of land in its vicinity. The Fort William–Port Arthur area also benefited from the CPR line in Northwestern Ontario. The growing number of workers involved in the transportation and shipping services provided by the twin towns stimulated agriculture so that by 1891 over 25,000 acres of land in the area were occupied.

The construction of the CPR was also responsible for the development of the rich agricultural lands in the Wabigoon district. Logging operations began in 1882 when the railway first passed through the area, providing the initial incentive for settlement, but it was not until the 1890s that farming developed on any significant scale. Largely responsible was the provincial minister of agriculture, John Dryden, an ardent booster of Northern Ontario's agricultural fortunes. Under Dryden's auspices, a provincial experimental farm was established at New Prospect in 1894. In the following year the townships of Van Horne and Wainwright and the townsite that would become Dryden were surveyed and opened to settlement.

In the mid-1890s the provincial government began an extensive advertising campaign, which included a booklet illustrating the agricultural advantages of Dryden. By 1897 the district had almost three hundred residents. These early arrivals faced countless hardships with little money or farming equipment. The farmers assisted each other, often donating food, clothing, and temporary accommodations to new arrivals. Cordwood, to be shipped to Winnipeg, was cut during the winter by most settlers in order to get additional income, and in the early years lumbering and gold-mining camps offered markets for agricultural produce.

An agricultural district whose development was unusual, as it occurred without the benefit of a railway connection, was the Little Clay Belt. One of the first settlers there was Charles C. Farr, a former Hudson's Bay Company clerk at Fort Temiskaming. By 1887 Farr had given up his post and established a farm and lumber operation at Humphrey's Depot, shortly to be renamed

6-14 *Sheep were an important part of the mixed-farm economy. The lambs were sold, and the wool went to mills for processing. Nels McRitchie (standing) oversees this flock at Devlin in 1905.*

6-15 *During the settlement period there was no major commercial egg or poultry production in the north. Most flocks were for domestic use; this flock of chickens and lone turkey were kept by Pierre de la Morandière in Killarney, 1921.*

6-16 *The draft team provided the pulling power on the farm before the arrival of the motorized tractor. This team on the Gold Eagle Farm, McKenzie Island, Red Lake district, belonged to Mary and Bill Naida (right). Joe Crysdale came along for the ride.*

6-14

6-15

6-16

Eagle Farm.

by him after his old school in England, Haileybury. Thanks to the reports of Farr and others extolling the agricultural, lumbering, and mining potential of the area, the provincial government began survey work in 1887. In 1891 five townships on the northwestern edge of Lake Timiskaming were opened to settlement at the price of fifty cents per acre, to be paid in instalments, and with conditions attached concerning clearance, cultivation, and house construction. Within two years Haileybury, with a post office, a grocery store, and other buildings, was the centre of a small but thriving farming community.

To facilitate the sale of lands and to supervise the settlement of the Little Clay Belt, in 1893 the provincial government appointed John Armstrong as land agent for the whole of the Lake Timiskaming area. Armstrong chose to establish his office away from Haileybury, at a location closer to the newly opened townships five miles north on Wabi Bay. This he called Liskeard, a name that later would be changed to New Liskeard to distinguish it from a similarly named village in Southern Ontario. Agricultural growth in the Little Clay Belt in these early years was slow because of difficulties of transportation and communication. In 1896 this isolation was partially eliminated with the completion of the CPR branch line from Mattawa to Lumbsden's Mill (Temiscamingue) on the Quebec side of Lake Timiskaming, though this still meant travelling by steamer across the lake to Haileybury. In 1900 a free excursion to the Haileybury–New Liskeard area, sponsored by the provincial government for 162 Southern Ontario farmers, resulted in 125 new homesteads being taken up. By 1901 the farming population of the area had surpassed one thousand.

With the exception of the Great Clay Belt, which still remained largely unpopulated, all of the other major agricultural areas in Northern Ontario were being settled by the beginning of the 20th century. Greatly assisting in this process were the land surveys carried out by private railway companies. As more and more reports appeared in the 1890s drawing attention to the vast wealth of timber, arable land, and minerals scattered across the north, the provincial government was motivated to commission a major resources survey of its own. In 1900 ten exploration parties were sent out across Northern Ontario, each composed of land surveyors, geologists, and land and timber evaluators. The optimistic tone of the reports of these teams provided the basis for the settlement and advertising policies followed by provincial governments during the next three decades.

One of the glaring weaknesses of the agricultural settlement pattern in Northeastern Ontario made apparent by the 1900 survey was the lack of railway access to two of the region's most promising farming districts, the Great and Little clay belts. To overcome this difficulty, in 1902 the Ross administration began construction of the Temiskaming and Northern Ontario Railway (T & NO) northward from North Bay as a provincially owned colonization road. The line reached New Liskeard in 1905 and Englehart in 1906, opening up the Little Clay Belt to greatly increased agricultural settlement. In addition, in the decade before World War I silver and gold mines went into production at Cobalt, South Porcupine, Elk Lake, and Gowganda, providing larger local markets to area farmers. Haileybury and New Liskeard particularly benefited in this way.

The T & NO was also crucial in the agricultural development of the Great Clay Belt; indeed, until the railroad reached Cochrane in 1908, farming was virtually nonexistent there. During the very early pre-war years, settlement was concentrated around Cochrane and Matheson, or along the railway between the two. By 1911, for example, the township of Glackmeyer to the immediate north of Cochrane had fifty lots occupied, with 216 acres in field crops and 2 acres of vegetables.

Equally important in the growth of agriculture in the Great Clay Belt was the completion of the National Transcontinental Railway in 1913. Passing through the heart of the Great Clay Belt, it resulted in a discontinuous spread of settlement from east to west, beginning in townships to the northeast of Cochrane, where it crossed the T & NO, through to Kapuskasing and Hearst. Government confidence in the agricultural potential of this area was demonstrated by the fact that in 1914 the

6-17 *The round barn with a ventilated cupola was an experimental design that appeared in various parts of Ontario in the early 20th century. Such buildings are now rare and are protected. This round barn was built by Fred Hawkes on the Kamstra farm in South Gillies in 1906. It was demolished in 1947; this is a 1942 view.*

6-18 *A horn of plenty: the produce of a home vegetable garden in the Rainy River Valley, proudly displayed at a fair in the early 1920s. The vegetables include pumpkin, squash, watermelon, cauliflower, sunflowers, and tomatoes.*

6-19 *The joy of sausage making: using an old-country recipe, this Kakabeka-area Dutch family makes one of its favourite foods. Served with erwtensoep and roggebrood (pea soup and rye bread), this worst would make an excellent meal. The unfortunate pig had probably grown up only a few feet away.*

6-17

6-18

6-19

federal Conservatives established an experimental farm at Kapuskasing, and in 1917 the provincial authorities did likewise at Hearst.

Successive provincial Conservative administrations also carried out intensive advertising campaigns in the first three decades of the 20th century to attract settlers to the clay belts. The colonization branch of the Department of Agriculture distributed 90,000 maps in 1908 and another 100,000 brochures in 1916, both times to good effect. These efforts were particularly successful with respect to the Little Clay Belt, as farming there expanded continuously until 1931, but were less so with regard to the Great Clay Belt. There the later 1920s witnessed the beginning of farm abandonment on a moderate scale.

Settlers moving into the clay belts were faced with many hardships. The lack of roads or even paths forced many to walk several miles through bush or around wet lands to arrive at their land. Most came with meagre means—perhaps an axe or a saw—but lacked basic equipment such as plows and wagons, and draft animals to haul timber, pull stumps, and break ground. Many pioneer settlers had to farm on a part-time basis, working the rest of the time on the railroad, or selling pulpwood or even hiring themselves out as hands to other farmers. Added to these hardships were other problems. The short growing season often resulted in crops being destroyed by early frosts or wet harvests. Fires used to burn brush and clear land sometimes went out of control, destroying the towns, farms, and forests in their way. Those of 1911, 1916, and 1922 were particularly devastating.

The expansion of agricultural settlement that took place in the clay belts in the first thirty years of the 20th century was repeated on a smaller scale in other farming communities in Northern Ontario. In the Sudbury area both the number of farms and the number of acres under cultivation steadily increased until 1921, when a consolidation of landholdings began to occur. Many of the farmers were French Canadians who had followed the lumbering industry into the district, as well as Finns and Ukrainians who immigrated to Canada in the years preceding World War I.

On Manitoulin Island the amount of acreage occupied continued to grow right up until 1950, although after 1930 the number of farms began to decline. After 1930, too, there was a shift to the raising of cattle, so that increases in acreage were due primarily to expanded fodder crops and pasture lands. In contrast, farming along the North Channel of Lake Huron has fluctuated more irregularly. Even before 1911 some farmsteads around Thessalon were abandoned, as yields decreased because of the sandy soil. Later many of these lands were used for pasture, until 1928 when a reforestation program was instituted. Elsewhere along the north shore the rural population increased steadily until 1911, as settlement followed the ribbons of the railways, the CPR, the Algoma Eastern, and the Algoma Central. World War I, however, brought a decline in the fortunes of farming in this region that continued throughout the 1920s.

In Northwestern Ontario the pattern of agricultural development in the 20th century has generally followed that of the northeast. With the growth of both Fort William and Port Arthur accelerated by the completion of the Canadian Northern main line to Winnipeg in 1901, farming in the Thunder Bay district also increased in importance. By 1911 there were 630 farms and nearly 110,000 acres of land in production in the area. Ten years later agricultural settlement was moving north and south of the Lakehead, along the Lake Superior shore to Nipigon Bay and the Pigeon River. The provincial government advertised the farming opportunities available, and this, combined with the industrialization of Fort William–Port Arthur in the 1920s, ensured continuous growth until the Great Depression.

In the smaller agricultural communities outside of the Thunder Bay region the story was much the same. In the Dryden area the number of farms doubled in the decade of the Great War and then increased a further 50 percent in the 1920s. Markets for farm produce were supplied by the workforce of the burgeoning pulp-and-paper industry established in 1913. Pulp and paper, along with lumbering, hydroelectricity, mining, and the building of the Canadian Northern Railway, were also responsible for the continued development of the Rainy River district. Population increases enticed increasing numbers of farmers to the area, so that by 1911 there were over 212,000 acres in production. This trend continued until 1931, unlike the trend in the Kenora region, where farm abandonment had already begun in the 1920s after agricultural settlement had peaked earlier in the decade.

The Great Depression was very much of a watershed in the history of Northern Ontario agriculture. In spite of concerted government efforts such as the Relief Land Settlement Scheme of 1932 to encourage settlement in the north, farm abandonment rather than expansion was the norm, and this trend has continued to the present. Since 1931, for example, the number of farms in Northern Ontario has dropped from 16,757 to 3,715 in 1981. Farm populations have also declined. During World War II many northerners enlisted, and once hostilities ended they were not interested in returning to farming. Then too, economies of scale involving larger operations and the use of fertilizer and machinery have had a negative impact. The 1950s ushered in a new era of mechanization and specialization. Tractor power replaced horsepower, and the family farm had to change from a subsistence to a commercial operation or wither and die. Other high-wage opportunities in mining and forestry have also reduced the farm population. In many areas farming has become a part-time operation, with the owner employed also in mining, pulp and paper, or lumbering.

Since 1931, the total acreage under production in Northern Ontario has fallen from 2,773,638 to 1,216,981 acres in 1981. About half of the remaining farms are commercial enterprises, with the greatest number in the Little Clay Belt, which leads the northern agricultural districts in total acreage, farm machinery, total farm value, and dairy cattle. The district of Kenora trails in these categories. Generally the emphasis throughout the north is on mixed farming, although dairy products supplying local urban centres contribute the major share of farm cash income. Crops of hay and oats predominate as livestock feed, and some specialty crops such as potatoes and poultry farming are found in certain districts. For the most part agriculture in the north serves local markets, though even here, competition from Southern Ontario and the United States has steadily eroded its development.

In the past half-century, agriculture has thus decreased significantly as an economic activity in Northern Ontario. That fact, however, should not be allowed to obscure the very important role that it has played in the history of the north. By overcoming the hardships and heartaches that they did, the early pioneer farmers contributed invaluably to the making of today's Ontario northland.

6–20

6-20 *Many farmers came to Northern Ontario from Quebec. Most of them settled from Mattawa northward along the clay belt to Cochrane; others settled from Mattawa to south of Lake Nipissing and along Lake Huron's north shore. Settlers arrived in the Noelville area in the 1890s. Pictured is the family of Napoléon Bouffard, 1918.*

6-21 *Blueberries, raspberries, and strawberries grew in abundance in many parts of the north. When preserved, they were an important supplement to the diet. Berry picking also provided a seasonal income for farm women and children. Here, members of the Sicotte and Despatie families display strawberries from Theodore Despatie's farm at Hanmer, 1931.*

6-21

6-22 *Garry Hanneman carries out forage tests at the New Liskeard demonstration farm in the 1950s. The farm was established in 1921 to encourage efficient farming practices in Northern Ontario and to carry out research projects. The New Liskeard College of Agricultural Technology had its beginnings in this program.*

6-23 *4-H (head, heart, hand, and health) Clubs have made a significant contribution to the development of agriculture. Club members must carry out an agricultural or homemaking task each year and are judged on their accomplishments. These 4-H members are a beef-judging team from Northeastern Ontario, competing at New Liskeard in 1958.*

6-22

6-23

124

6-24 *Dairies, creameries, and cheese factories*
6-25 *sprang up in the dairy-farming areas of Northern Ontario to process the milk and distribute their products to consumers. 6-24, William Daoust's cheese factory in 1914. 6-25, the Thunder Bay Co-op Dairy in Port Arthur, probably in the 1930s. The company's motto was "You can whip our cream, but you can't beat our milk."*

6-26 *Probably the last sectors of the agriculture industry to give up using horse power were the dairies and bakeries, in their door-to-door delivery routes. C. Bois and his steed delivered milk for the Espanola Dairy in the 1920s.*

6-24

6-26

6-25

6-27 *Beef cattle were sold in auctions at sale barns, in places such as Thessalon and Little Current. Some were purchased by travelling drovers and brought to a central stockyard for rail shipment to southern slaughterhouses. This is the CPR stockyard at North Bay, around 1900.*

6-28 *Small market gardens and greenhouse operations have begun to serve the growing urban population, which no longer grows its own kitchen produce. Lily Lum worked on a market-gardening operation in the Sudbury area in 1944.*

6-29 *Bee-keeping, both as a hobby and as a source of fresh honey, is popular in Northern Ontario. However, the northern climate makes it difficult to operate a commercial apiary—spring often comes too late and the summers are too dry. Here, Frank Foster keeps a protected eye on his bees in Thornloe, 1917.*

6-30 *The farmers' outdoor market in Timmins, 1938. These markets benefited both the producer and the consumer. Without the middle stages of large distribution centres and supermarkets, the costs were kept down and the produce reached the table "farm fresh."*

6-27

6-28

6-29

6-30

126

CHAPTER SEVEN

Industry

C.M. WALLACE
Associate Professor of History,
Laurentian University,
Sudbury.

7-1 *A ship under construction, possibly at the*
Port Arthur shipyards during World War I.
The Western Drydock and Shipbuilding
Co. opened its plant in the city in 1911.

7–2 *The locks at Sault Ste. Marie, Michigan, at the turn of the century. Good water-transportation routes were a mixed blessing for the industrial development of Northern Ontario. It was quite economical to move raw materials to the south for processing, so there was little incentive to establish manufacturing facilities in the north.*

7–3 *The Soo Dredging and Construction Co. expanded Algoma Steel's ore docks in 1914.*

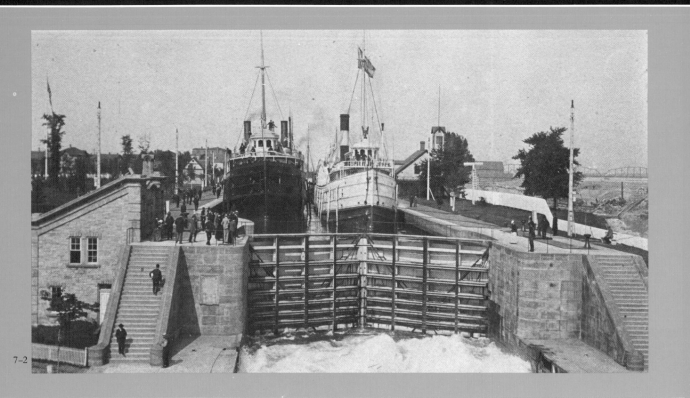

7–2

7–3

7–4 The first transcontinental train out of Fort William leaves the Westfort roundhouse on June 30, 1886. The industrial development of the Lakehead, and of Northern Ontario generally, coincided with the construction and completion of the rail lines.

7–5 Roast yards at Copper Cliff, about 1890. The Sudbury area's mineral wealth consisted of combinations of iron, copper, and nickel sulphides. To remove the sulphur from the ore, the ore was piled on a foundation of wood sufficient to maintain a fire for about 60 hours. The sulphur might continue to burn for three or four months, until all but 10% of the sulphur was removed. Unfortunately, the sulphurous fumes

destroyed local vegetation and made farming difficult. Subsequent mining-industry and government environmental measures have vastly improved the situation.

7–4

7–5

7-6 *The Iroquois Falls paper mill was built between 1913 and 1915, after Frank Anson and Shirley Ogilvie gained the right to cut wood along the Abitibi River. Construction was difficult because there was no road connecting the mill to the rail line, six miles away. Eventually the Abitibi Power and Paper Co. fell under American control.*

7–6

THE "TREASURE CHEST OF CANADA," as Ontario called its north, was early recognized by the province as an "inexhaustible resource" for the industrial heartland to the south. Turn-of-the-century governments, hoping to unlock the chest and control the wealth, acted aggressively by imposing the "manufacturing condition" on developers. As a result, large investments in sawmills and pulp-and-paper mills flowed into the north. A similar attempt to control mining failed, and eventually the complex industrial pattern that emerged in Ontario drew northern resources south, along with the associated employment, income, and profits.

The abundant waterways and railroads that opened the north and linked its communities were, at once, both a blessing and a curse. In the early years this cheap transportation encouraged northern growth and expansion; in later years the advantages of processing closer to markets and the industrialized core meant that unprocessed raw materials were shipped out, leaving the "hewers of wood and drawers of water" in the north acutely aware of their position. The population of the north, spread out and sparse, never became large enough to encourage more than cottage industries, with a few notable exceptions.

The manufacturing that does take place across the north is usually for local consumption. Eplett, Kellough, and Klomp-Wakefield dairies produce milk and cream for their local markets. Scollie's ice cream is as much appreciated in the northwest as Thornloe cheese is in the northeast. Northern Breweries, formerly Doran's, survived the takeover and shutdown attempt of the metropolitan brewing interests and retains a faithful clientele both in the north and outside of it. The larger cities, North Bay, Timmins, Sudbury, Sault Ste. Marie, and Thunder Bay, have all developed industrial sectors to varying degrees, especially in the service areas, but only Thunder Bay can claim to have a diversified economy producing finished goods for external markets.

The several moves by Sir John A. Macdonald's national Liberal-Conservative party, with its designs for "Canada for the Canadians" in 1879, began the modern era in the north. Industry was to be protected by the National Policy, and a transcontinental railway was to tie the country and the market together. The daring and expensive decision to build a line across Northern Ontario, in the face of Liberal opposition, permitted the urban-industrialized communities to rise in the wilderness. The completion of construction in 1885 signalled a new departure in the north. That year, copper mines were being planned in Sudbury.

Samuel J. Ritchie, an American speculator, was among the first to grasp the potential of the Sudbury Basin. With himself as president, he had the Canadian Copper Company incorporated in 1886, with headquarters in Cleveland, Ohio. Copper was the lure that attracted Ritchie, but in Sudbury it was mined in a compound with "devil's copper" or nickel, for which no commercial process to separate copper from nickel then existed. The discovery of a nickel-separation technique in the 1880s and the recognition of a use for nickel as an alloy produced the first large-scale industrial development based on the resources of Northern Ontario. With Germany, Britain, and the United States enlarging their navies, the hardened steel produced by the addition of nickel found a market.

The Canadian Copper Company was not alone in Sudbury. A Swiss entrepreneur, Ludwig Mond, obtained mineral rights as well and began building a mining-smelting complex to serve the European market. A non-military use of nickel was demonstrated by the Massey-Harris Company of Toronto, which entranced viewers at the Chicago World's Fair of 1893 with the nickel-plated parts on its farm machinery. As the demand for nickel expanded, the roast heaps around Copper Cliff, where Ritchie's company carried out the first stage of preparing the ore, grew into small mountains. The ground-level sulphur fumes quickly destroyed the vegetation in the region and blackened the rocks after the topsoil was washed away. When the fires died, the copper and nickel were removed and sent to New Jersey or Wales for further processing.

Ritchie soon found himself outmanoeuvred as head of the Canadian Copper Company, and in 1902 the American banker J.P. Morgan incorporated the International Nickel Company, gaining control of the Canadian Copper Company and the New Jersey refinery. Sudbury matte continued to be shipped to the United States for refining and was then sold internationally. The naval building race in Europe continued until 1914, driving Sudbury's nickel output from 5,945 tons in 1902 up to 24,838 in 1913. That was 75 percent of the world's market. By 1918 Sudbury's share grew to 90 percent.

During these years another American promoter was creating a spectacular industrial empire at Sault Ste. Marie. Until Francis Hector Clergue arrived in 1894, that town had remained relatively obscure, even though it was located at the critical intersection of the upper Great Lakes. Clergue rescued the town from the $263,000 debt it had incurred in constructing an electric power plant, and over the next eight years he created an industrial com-

plex with few parallels in Canada. After enlarging the power plant, he built the Sault Ste. Marie Pulp and Paper Company, which used the power to convert the abundant local spruce into 150 tons of pulp daily by 1896. Clergue's company perfected a machine to dry the pulp, and then he built a sulphite paper mill in 1898. The need for sulphuric acid took him to the Canadian Copper Company in Sudbury, from whom he tried to purchase waste sulphur. When he was rebuffed, he acquired his own mineral rights and produced both nickel and sulphur. Experiments with new techniques led to a contract with Krupp, the large German steel company, which resulted in the construction of a ferro-nickel plant in the Sault. A nearby alkali property made chlorine, which was used as bleach in the pulp-and-paper mill.

Meanwhile, Clergue bought an iron-ore deposit in the Michipicoten region and opened the Helen Mine, which became the most productive in Ontario. To deliver the ore to the Sault he started construction of the Algoma Central Railway in 1899. By 1900 it was carrying ore twelve miles to his harbour at Michipicoten, for shipment south on Algoma Central's lake freighters. Clergue hoped to use all of this ore in his own operations, though he originally shipped to the lower Great Lakes and the United States. He was soon into his next phase, the creation of the Algoma Iron, Nickel, and Steel Company, incorporated in 1901. The Bessemer converter went into operation in 1902; by then, Clergue's Sault Ste. Marie interests included sawmills, brick plants, machine shops, ferries, a foundry, and a car shop. It is doubtful that a more fully integrated operation than the Lake Superior Corporation existed in Canada in 1902. The Clergue story up to this point clearly indicated that Northern Ontario could support diversified secondary industry. His company, unfortunately, was bankrupt.

Clergue's dynamism as a developer was not matched by skills in management, marketing, or long-range financing. He was unable to raise more capital to finance his ambitious projects. Perhaps the Morgan empire engineered his failure, as was rumoured, or perhaps competitors such as the United States Steel Company ran him out

7-7 Francis Hector Clergue originated the modern industrial city in Sault Ste. Marie. He built a system of mines, railways, and mills that eventually emerged as the Algoma Steel Corp., Abitibi Power and Paper Co., Algoma Central Railway, and Great Lakes Power Co. However, in 1903 he went bankrupt, throwing 3,500 men out of work. The Ontario government stepped in to rescue some of the businesses, and many years later Clergue was invited back to Sault Ste. Marie and hailed as one of the founders of the city.

7-8 The Helen iron ore mines near Michipicoten,
7-9 the Algoma Central Railway, and Michipicoten harbour were essential to the success of Francis Clergue's industries in Sault Ste. Marie. 7-8 is Michipicoten harbour, probably in the 1950s. 7-9 is the harbour in the early 1900s.

7-7

7-8

7-9

7-10 *All industries require some form of power, whether from water, steam, or hydroelectricity. Kakabeka Falls was tapped for hydroelectric-power generation around 1905. These Kam Power Co. workers are building the forebay of the dam for the project.*

7-11 *The Ontario-Minnesota Pulp and Paper Mill was completed in 1914. The strong American demand for newsprint and Ontario tariff laws forced many U.S. firms to open mills in Northern Ontario; before that time the pulpwood was shipped south. This firm, now owned by Boise Cascade Canada Ltd., remains the largest employer in Fort Frances.*

7-12 *Clergue incorporated the Algoma Iron, Nickel and Steel Co. in 1901, about the same time that these coke ovens were being built for the company.*

7-11

7-10

7-12

of business. Whatever the case, Clergue was soon on his way to Europe and new ventures, leaving the government and other corporations to pick up the pieces.

The collapse of Clergue's empire in 1903 demonstrated the fragility of industry in the north. It also had its victims; the workers made the first sacrifices. About 3,500 were put out of work immediately, with a hollow promise that they would be paid. A few weeks later, supplies ran out in the bush camps. Workers from the woods as well as the town descended on the company offices, only to be informed that there was no money and that they should look for work elsewhere. The riot that followed spread through the town. Company employees, trapped on the second floor of their building, resorted to firing guns "to keep out the rioters." The city militia was called out, and four hundred soldiers were brought in from Toronto to control the "reckless" lumberjacks. Labour relations in the north did not get off to a healthy start. The Ontario government had a more constructive approach; it decided to put the Clergue empire back into operation under a new president, C.D. Warren, who slowly put it on its feet.

Clergue's success at the Sault had far-reaching effects on Northern Ontario's industrial development. At the Lakehead, where sawmilling and mine-supplying had begun in the 1860s, Clergue's achievements caused a great deal of envy and led to unrelenting efforts in both Fort William and Port Arthur to secure industrial investment. These efforts had only limited success. The Ogilvie flour mill was established in Fort William in 1904, and in 1907 the short-lived Atikokan Iron Company opened in Port Arthur. A continuing Lakehead industry began with the establishment of the Western Drydock and Shipbuilding Company in Port Arthur in 1910-11. Begun by a local entrepreneur, James Whalen, the company was financed by American capital. It was followed in 1912 by the establishment of a Fort William plant of the Canadian Car and Foundry Company, destined to become one of Canada's major producers of railway and subway cars.

Industrial development in the Rat Portage–Keewatin area initially resulted from the partnership of Canadian

enterprise. In the late 1870s John Mather established his Keewatin Lumber and Manufacturing Company to supply lumber and railway ties for railway construction between the Lakehead and Red River. He then joined Alexander Mitchell, a Montreal grain merchant, in establishing the Lake of the Woods Milling Company. The large mill near the CPR track later inspired Frederick Philip Grove to turn from agrarian subjects and chronicle an industrial family and the insurance fraud on which its wealth was based, in his novel, *The Master of the Mill*.

These examples of 19th-century industrial development were matched after the turn of the century by the many companies set up to exploit Northern Ontario's forests. The primary force was the Ontario government, which became convinced during the 1890s that far too much Ontario wood was being processed in the United States and that Michigan mills would saw Canadian logs as long as they were allowed to do so. Premier A.S. Hardy's Liberal government therefore imposed a "manufacturing condition" on Ontario woodworking in 1898, compelling the American companies to move their operations across Lake Huron. Hardy's determination to end the depradations of these "thieves and plunderers" was extended in 1900 to the cutting of spruce pulpwood on Crown lands.

Pulp mills were established at Sturgeon Falls in 1901 and at Espanola in 1905, and the first in Northwestern Ontario were built at Fort William and Dryden in 1911. Then, as the United States Congress responded to the pressure for cheaper newsprint and reduced the pulpwood tariff to almost nothing, the mills really began to spring up: at Iroquois Falls in 1912, Fort Frances in 1914, Smooth Rock Falls in 1917, Port Arthur in 1918 (a fine-paper mill), Kapuskasing and Timiskaming in 1920, Haileybury and Nipigon in 1921, and Kenora in 1924. Additional mills were built at Fort William in 1924 and at Port Arthur in 1926.

These pulp-and-paper developments, which neither war economy nor postwar depression seemed to hinder, brought about what historian A.R.M. Lower has called "another industrial revolution." Since mills required large sources of power, the construction of a mill was often accompanied by the building of large waterpower facilities. As a result, although there was some municipal generation of power, most hydroelectric generation in Northern Ontario was owned by the pulp-and-paper companies. These resources were an additional source of profit for these companies, reflected in the proud title of the Abitibi Power and Paper Company, incorporated in 1914. This company, which had its beginnings in the efforts of Shirley Ogilvie of the Montreal flour-milling family, began the development of forest resources well north of the Lakes when it built a mill at Iroquois Falls. Eventually, however, Abitibi fell under American control.

The "manufacturing condition" forced on American investment in the forest-products industries in Northern Ontario could not be imposed on nickel refining. The mineral resources were already out of Crown control, and the hostility of the United States government encouraged those nickel producers controlled by International Nickel to resist Ontario's demands that the ore be refined in the province. After the outbreak of World War I Canadians became concerned that nickel refined in the neutral United States might find its way to the enemy, yet International Nickel stubbornly refused to yield.

The Ontario government established the Royal Ontario Nickel Commission in 1916 to investigate the problem, but the issue was not forced until reports surfaced of the submarine *Deutschland* carrying nickel from New York to Germany. International Nickel finally decided to build a refinery in Ontario, but chose to locate it at Port Colborne on Lake Erie. The Ontario government then imposed a new mining tax aimed directly at International Nickel. The $1.3 million of back taxes marked the "culmination of years of bitterness against the company and its policies, and probably also the desire to divert some of the war profits of a foreign corporation in Ontario."

The era of war production and postwar crisis demonstrated some new realities of Northern Ontario industry. A recession that had begun in 1913 was ended by the demands of the war. Munitions were manufactured in Fort William, and naval vessels in Port Arthur. Algoma Steel, however, was less successful in adapting its steel output to munitions production. Nickel production at Sudbury reached unprecedented heights, and pulp-and-paper production struggled to meet the combined Canadian and American demand. The depression that followed the war forced adjustments everywhere. Northern Ontarians were beginning to face the problems of alternating periods of soaring prosperity and ravaging depression produced by the boom-and-bust cycle that marked the resource frontier. By the mid-1920s most of Northern Ontario was back in production.

Good times had returned to Sudbury after plant closures in 1922. The demand for stainless steel, especially for the automobile and electrical appliance manufacturers, finally created a steady peacetime demand for nickel. Wartime production levels were surpassed in the late 1920s, as International Nickel acquired the Mond Nickel Company in 1929 and became even more dominant in the area. However, the company did not quite have a monopoly. Falconbridge Nickel was incorporated in 1928, and in 1930 it began to develop the Edison property.

The experiences of the pulp-and-paper companies were initially similar to those of the nickel companies. Faced with a surging demand for paper that yielded ever-larger production and profits, Abitibi decided in 1928 to expand its control across the Canadian Shield. It acquired the Spanish River Pulp and Paper Mills and bought the Fort William Power Company as well as the Thunder Bay Paper Company. It eventually extended its control, through subsidiaries, from eastern Manitoba to the lower St. Lawrence River. The closing of the Espanola mill at the end of 1929 was part of the rationalization of its empire, but as the Great Depression drove demand down the company was forced into receivership in 1932, when it could not even pay interest on its bonds. Not until 1946 did Abitibi break out of receivership, although some production had continued under the receiver's management.

The Depression produced great contrasts in industrial experience. At the depths in 1932, nickel production plummeted to 28,000 short tons, but an upward trend in world consumption that started the following year led to

7–13

7–14

7–15

7-16 *The 10th convention of the Lumber Workers Industrial Union of Canada at Port Arthur, 1934. The year before, employers had broken a strike by the union.*

7-17 *These men worked on the building of the Abitibi Marine Base at Orient Bay in 1937-38. The base organized the transportation of logs to the Abitibi mills at the Lakehead.*

7-18 *The constant expansion of the pulp-and-paper industry demanded more hydroelectric power. Here, turbine forms are installed at Cameron Falls, 1918.*

7-16

7-17

7-18

an increase in production at a rate of about 20,000 short tons annually. European and Japanese industries were the major buyers, and by 1935 Inco and Falconbridge were both at full production, hiring more workers and adding new capacity as quickly as possible. As world nickel production reached 162,500 tons in 1939, the Sudbury Basin not only missed most of the Depression but also drew the unemployed from across the nation.

In Sault Ste. Marie, Algoma Steel had a more difficult time of it. The company overcame its production problems during the 1920s only to find itself in receivership in 1932. Three years later, James Dunn, in "Canada's most daring industrial coup" up to that time, gained control of a $75 million company for less than $10 million. He managed to show a profit of a half-million dollars within a year and continued to increase Algoma's assets to $109 million and annual profits to $10 million by the time he died in 1956.

These capitalist achievements contrasted sharply with the experience of most Northern Ontario workers. Some of the prosperity in the Sudbury Basin and the goldmining communities trickled down to the workers, but their attempts to organize unions and to improve working conditions met with harsh opposition from their employers. The CPR used every means to disrupt union-organization efforts by its freight handlers in Fort William around 1910. Cobalt miners had formed a union in 1919, but it was shattered in a strike that the mine owners resisted. Pulpwood cutters in the Thunder Bay area struck for recognition of their Lumber Workers' Industrial Union in 1933, only to see their leaders "arrested on charges of assault, unlawful assembly and riding trains without paying fares." A year later the pulpwood cutters around Sault Ste. Marie struck for recognition and met with the same reaction. In 1935 over two thousand loggers at Nipigon struck for improved living conditions and better wages, again without success.

The outbreak of war in 1939 provided Northern Ontario industry with a new start. All sectors of the economy were back in full production in 1940, although there were severe restrictions on prices and wages. These inhibited the recovery of the pulp-and-paper industry, but the nickel and steel industries expanded employment, production, and profits. Lakehead industries also boomed during these years. The Canadian Car and Foundry Company built the first of many Hawker Hurricanes in 1942, a dramatic leap into the ranks of secondary industry. The Port Arthur shipyards struggled to keep up with orders. No doubt C.D. Howe, MP for Port Arthur and minister of munitions and supply, was pleased with the industrial activity in his riding.

Union organization in this era was more successful than before. The United Steelworkers organized the Algoma workers in the Sault, the Mine, Mill union organized the miners and smelter workers of the Sudbury Basin, and other unions were busy at the Lakehead. The federal government supported these efforts, recognizing that after the war new economic-planning and labour-relations approaches would be needed to prevent the boom-and-bust cycles that had plagued the whole country. It attempted to prevent strikes during the war; the goldminers' strike at Kirkland Lake in 1941-42 was one of the few exceptions. The owners and managers of northern industry did not share the government's new attitude and failed to adopt the federal acceptance of union organization. Among the most rabidly anti-union men in the country before the war, they did not change their attitudes during it. Not surprisingly, their employees became some of the most militant union members in Canada after the war.

No depression followed World War II. There was a short readjustment period, but factories converted to peacetime output were soon producing at capacity levels. The large American demand for raw materials, especially minerals, helped to fuel an upward swing that continued with minor interruptions into the 1970s. The pulp-and-paper industry, using new techniques that pulped jack pine, began to expand again. New mills were built at Red Rock in 1944, Marathon in 1945, and Terrace Bay in 1948, and a second mill was built at North Bay in 1957. However, British Columbia now became an aggressive pulp-and-paper producer, and Ontarians began to find themselves working antiquated mills in a more competitive market. Some plants closed, but others gained a new lease on life by renovating their plants, adopting automated technology, and diversifying their operations.

During this "golden age" of industrial expansion some Northern Ontarians developed expectations that would later appear grandiose, even outrageous. The Lakehead cities led in industrial expansion; by 1956, 211 manufacturing establishments produced goods valued at over $170 million, triple the total for 1946. Ships, buses, and aircraft were built there in their entirety. Canadian Car produced almost six hundred units for the Montreal transit system in the late 1950s. Both the Toronto Transit Commission and the GO train system ordered more cars. The company also built de Havilland parts and complete Harvard T6 aircraft for the Department of Defence. The Port Arthur Shipbuilding Company built minesweepers for the navy and icebreakers for the Department of Transport. Husky Oil opened a refinery, and several chemical plants were built to service the pulp-and-paper mills. No other community in Northern Ontario could match the Lakehead's diversity in these years.

The other cities also had their industrial achievements. Sault Ste. Marie grew as Algoma Steel expanded its product lines and capacity. Employment grew dramatically until the steel market collapsed around 1980. The company has had its share of industrial disputes, however; the 1946 strike was the first of several intense struggles.

Sudbury also experienced a good deal of industrial warfare. A slight recession in the late 1950s led to the first and only Mine, Mill strike against International Nickel. Lasting several months during the fall and winter of 1958, the strike all but crippled the union, led to a change in leadership, and enabled the United Steelworkers to challenge the Mine, Mill union successfully at International Nickel, though not at Falconbridge. Sudbury then became the site of some of the longest and most costly strikes in Canadian history. The United Steelworkers against International Nickel, international union against multinational corporation, set a pattern for the province. The prosperity of the industry was a factor, as nickel

remained in high demand and production expanded time and again. Even though new equipment and technology were incorporated with each alteration, employment remained high (International Nickel alone employed over 20,000 workers) until supply began to exceed demand in the late 1970s and automation displaced thousands of workers.

Smaller centres also became industrialized to some extent after the war. North Bay, a transportation and service centre in earlier decades, began to attract industry in the 1950s. Earlier industries were two mining industry suppliers, Canadian Longyear Limited, a manufacturer of diamond-core drills in North Bay since 1930, and the Craig Bit Company, which began making steel bits there in 1941. Dupont of Canada and the Canadian Johns-Manville Company both moved into North Bay in 1957. Dupont began producing explosives, largely for the mining industry, while Johns-Manville manufactured insulating board.

In two other towns, Ontario government policy was an important factor. At Timmins, where Texasgulf developed the Kidd Creek Mine in 1964, the company built a zinc smelter eight years later and added a copper smelter when an Ontario tax incentive program made it more economical to smelt the ore in Ontario. The "manufacturing condition" had eventually made an impact on mining. At Elliot Lake, where uranium mining had almost ended about 1960, Ontario Hydro's plunge into nuclear energy later in the decade made the community a boom town again. The Eldorado refinery at Blind River will process Elliot Lake's uranium.

Except for Thunder Bay, none of the industrial towns of Northern Ontario has a very broad base. The single-resource community, vulnerable to the loss or depletion of its resource or its market, is classic Northern Ontario. This was recognized in the early 1970s by the provincial government; its 1971 *Design for Development* report declared that "The region as a whole has a narrow and relatively slow-growing economic base. This is the case in most of the larger centres and is particularly so in the many smaller communities. If, under these conditions, the dominant industry declines, substantial hardships follow because few, if any, alternative forms of employment are available."

A 1969 conference at Lakehead University introduced the concept of a Mid-Canada Development Corridor. That dream is unlikely to be realized; *Design for Development* appears to be a more realistic assessment of the state of affairs. The provincial government has done much to encourage small business, service industries, and tourism through agencies such as the Northern Ontario Development Corporation. Sudbury has demonstrated its ability to survive Inco shutdowns and the loss of mining jobs, evidence of the vitality of other kinds of business. Another government agency, the Urban Transportation Development Corporation, has assumed control of the Canadian Car plant in Thunder Bay and strengthened its competition in the world's market for light-transit vehicles. Government involvement in Northern Ontario's industrial development remains significant.

7-19

7-20

7-21 *Railway ties were impregnated with creosote preservative at the Canadian Creosoting Co. in Sudbury, 1947. The ties were piled in this large vat, the door was tightly latched, and the creosote was forced into the vat under very high pressure.*

7-22 *Cleaning a paper-making machine at the Spruce Falls Power and Paper Co., Kapuskasing, 1946.*

7-23 *After the war industrial production did not slump, but the products changed. Algoma Steel manufactured rails. Part of the process was called "gagging the rail," ensuring that the rail was straight. Charles Ray and James Moss performed this job in 1950.*

7-24 *A wood-veneer machine operation at the Weldwood Veneer plant, Longlac, 1968.*

7-25 *Many smaller, secondary industries sprang up in the north after World War II. These women worked on the cupboard-assembly production line at the Hill Clark Francis Mill in New Liskeard, 1947.*

7-26 *Sanding skis at a manufacturing plant in Sudbury, 1947.*

7–21

7–22

7–23

7–24

7–25

7–26

7-27 *Although commercial fishing has declined in importance, it was one of Northern Ontario's earliest industries. Here a fisherman dip-nets a catch of lake trout and whitefish off South Baymouth, Manitoulin Island, 1949.*

7-28 *Roy Crane of Cat Lake loads ice onto the fish at a Windigo fish plant, about 1980.*

7-29 *At the beginning of the 20th century almost all fur farms raised fox. By the time this photograph of a mink farm in South Gillies was made in the 1940s, fashions had changed and over 90% of fur farms raised mink.*

7-30 *North Bay has become a major centre in Canada's fur industry. These men are grading pelts before a fur auction in the 1970s.*

7-27

7-28

7-29

7-30

7–31 *The paper mill at Dryden, 1960s. In 1983 the new owner, Great Lakes Forest Products, was completing a huge expansion program, with improvements including pollution controls and the replacement of both machinery and systems.*

7–32 *The paper-making machinery at E.B. Eddy's Espanola mill, during an MLA tour in 1972.*

7–33 *The paper mill at Espanola was completed in 1905. The town and mill prospered together, until the Depression turned the area into a ghost town. The mill housed German prisoners of war during World War II and was reopened as a mill by the Kalamazoo Vegetable Parchment Co. after the war. It is now operated by E.B. Eddy and produces fine paper and specialized paper products.*

7–34 *Checking rolls of newsprint at the Abitibi mill, 1952.*

7–31

7–32

7–33

7–34

7-35 *Thunder Bay harbour in 1982. Thunder Bay is the world's largest grain-handling port; in 1983 the harbour handled almost 26 million tons, much of it grain from the prairies.*

7-36 *Algoma Steel's operations in Sault Ste. Marie have made the city Canada's second-largest steel centre. This is the steel-making plant, looking west, in the early 1980s.*

7-35

7-36

7-37 *The Super Stack at Inco's Copper Cliff smelter is as high as the Empire State Building at 1,250 ft. The community's greening efforts are visible at the foreground of this picture.*

7-38 *Producing metals for the world calls for state-of-the-art technology. At Inco's Copper Cliff mill, computerized equipment was installed to monitor many operations, including the pyrrhotite rejection circuit.*

7-38

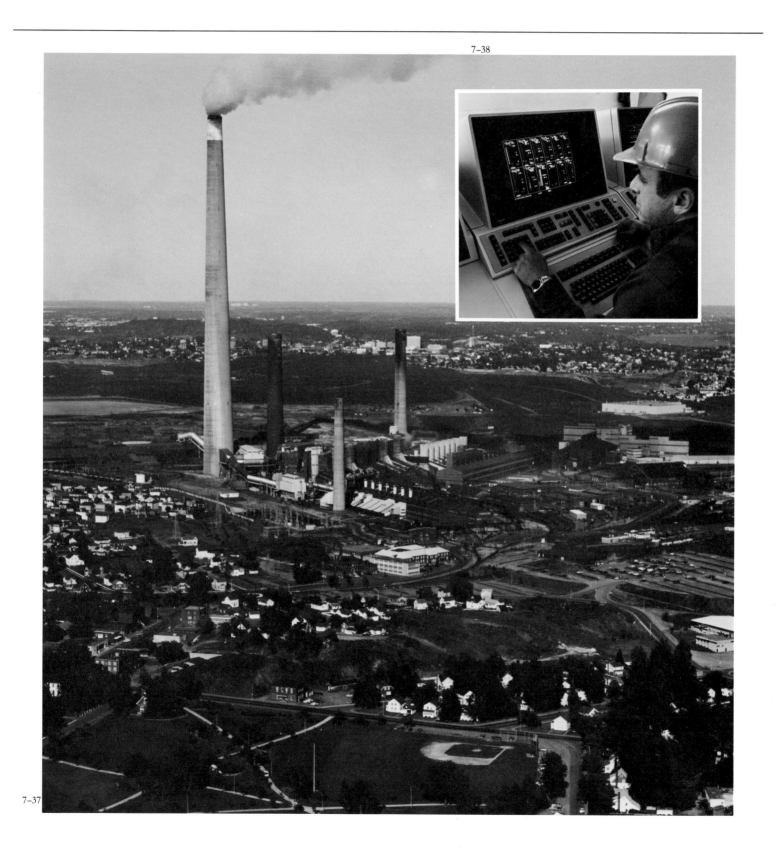

7-37

CHAPTER EIGHT

Cities and Towns

OIVA SAARINEN
Associate Professor of Geography,
Laurentian University,
Sudbury.

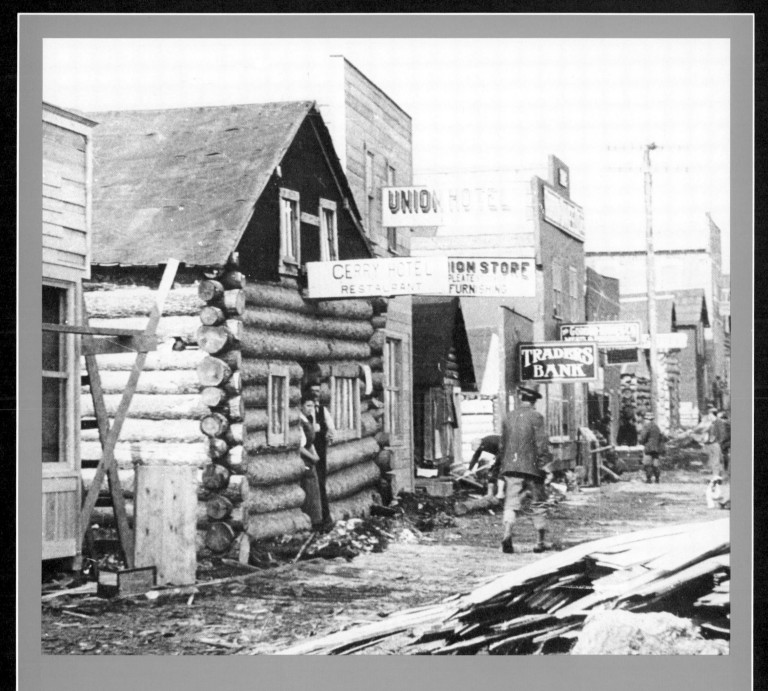

8-1 *Golden City, now Porcupine, was much
like other boom towns before 1910—built
from the trees that had been cut down to
make room for the mines. The most common
buildings were hotels, banks, and restaurants.*

8-2 *Immigrant sheds at Port Arthur, around 1890. Prince Arthur's Landing had earlier been a staging area for water transportation to Canada's northwest. With the construction of the CPR in the 1880s, the newly named Port Arthur became a stopover for immigrants, who stayed in these quarters before travelling west by train.*

8-3 *Sault Ste. Marie was an important staging point during the fur-trade years, a major steamboat landing point at the turn of this century, and is now an integral link in the St. Lawrence Seaway system. At the time this photograph was taken, around 1900, it was growing rapidly as a result of industrial development.*

8-4 *James and John Dawson stand in the doorway of Sault Ste. Marie's prestigious Dawson Block, 1898. The building housed not only their grocery store, but also the Odd Fellows' Lodge, which met on alternate Tuesdays, and a consulting engineer.*

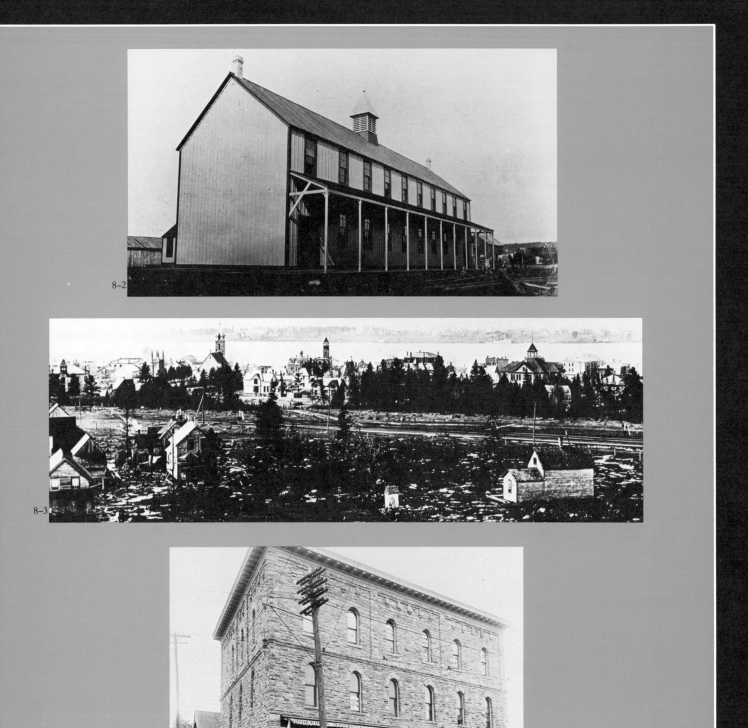

8-2

8-3

8-4

8-5 *Shortly after silver was found at Cobalt in 1903, tents, shacks, and cabins appeared. By 1908 the town's population had mushroomed to 7,000. Basic services accompanied the growth; there were 18 hotels, 6 churches, 4 banks, 2 schools, a courthouse, and a jail. A fast-food wagon in this photo offers "Quick Lunch."*

8-6 *The Real Porcupine Co. was one of the many services available to Porcupine's residents around 1912. The man in the window is inspecting a piece of ore that will undoubtedly make him wealthy beyond his wildest dreams.*

8-7 *Little England, a boxcar community housing English immigrant railway workers and their families at Ignace, around 1910. The wooden fence separates the houses from the CPR tracks.*

8-5

8-6

8-7

149

8-8 *Timmins was incorporated as a town in*
8-9 *1912. 8-8, houses under construction when*
Timmins was "six weeks old and already 63
houses." 8-9, Timmins's residential area
before World War I, looking northeast from
the water tower.

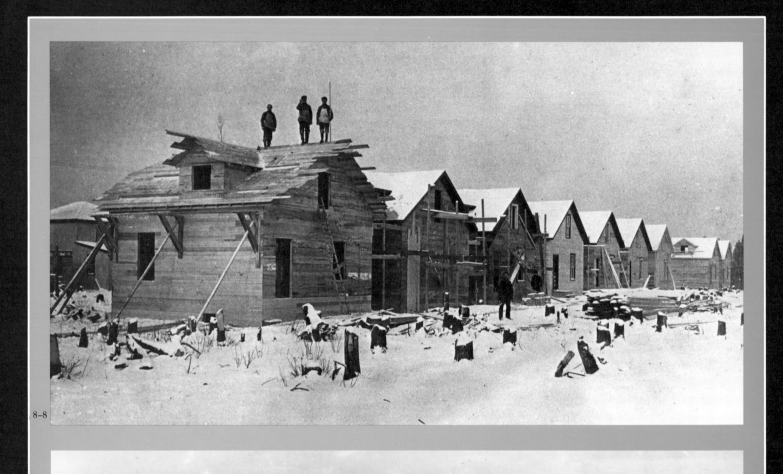

8-8

8-9

T HE URBAN HISTORY of Northern Ontario has differed markedly from that elsewhere in Canada. Urbanization here occurred comparatively late, so that most cities and towns are little more than a century old. Indeed, not until World War II did more than half of the north's population live in officially designated urban centres, and even today the north lags behind the rest of the province in this respect. In contrast to Southern Ontario, too, Northern Ontario possesses no large metropolis. Consequently small and medium-sized centres, many of which are single-enterprise resource communities, have a much greater relative importance here than elsewhere in the province.

The pattern of urban settlement since Confederation has been that of a general progression northward and westward from the fringes of Lake Huron and Lake Superior. In 1871 Bruce Mines, with a population of 1,300, was the largest settlement in the north, although in the following decade it declined when its copper mines were abandoned. Settlement at Sault Ste. Marie was tied closely to the rapids on the St. Marys River, eighteen miles below its source at Lake Superior. Long a Roman Catholic mission and fur-trading post, the "Soo's" modern era began in 1855 with the construction of an American canal system to bypass the rapids. In 1861 it was designated a free port, and a decade later its population had climbed to 900. In Northwestern Ontario the village of Nipigon (population 500), located at the mouth of the Nipigon River, had grown up around the Hudson's Bay Company's Red Rock trading post.

During the 1870s new settlements came into existence and old ones expanded. Mattawa, a long-time missionary and fur-trading post at the junction of the Mattawa and Ottawa rivers, began to develop as a booming lumber community, as did Thessalon and Blind River, both located on the North Channel of Lake Huron. Then, too, the Thunder Bay area began to reclaim the importance it had enjoyed during the fur-trade era at the beginning of the century. Two rival communities were located in the Thunder Bay area. Prince Arthur's Landing, situated at the eastern end of the Dawson Road to Manitoba, was also accessible to the Silver Islet mining development. A few miles to the west, near the mouth of the Kaministikwia River, stood Fort William, smaller than its neighbour and consisting of little more than a Hudson's Bay Company post. Fort William's fortunes improved in 1875, when the federal government designated it the Lake Superior terminus of the transcontinental railway. Not to be outdone, Prince Arthur's Landing built a connecting link to the new railroad in 1878. The economies of the two towns were also bolstered by the burgeoning lumber industry in the region. By 1881 their combined populations approached 2,000, and expectations were high that the Lakehead would become a major transshipment point.

The pace of urban development quickened during the 1880s and 1890s, particularly as a result of the construction of the Canadian Pacific Railway (CPR). Prince Arthur's Landing became Port Arthur in 1882, when the CPR chose the community as its main Lakehead station. In 1884 the first terminal grain elevator was constructed at Fort William, and the first shipment of Manitoba wheat to eastern markets passed through it. In the same year Port Arthur received its town charter. After a dispute over municipal taxation in 1889, however, the CPR concentrated its grain- and freight-handling facilities in Fort William.

Both communities grew steadily in the 1890s. In 1892 Fort William was incorporated as a town, and Port Arthur established an electric street-railway system, one of the first municipally built, owned, and operated systems in North America. This system was soon extended to Fort William, which was developing as an important distribution point for the mining-exploration and lumbering industries in the Thunder Bay area. Port Arthur's fortunes in turn were boosted in 1901, when it was chosen as the Lake Superior terminus for the Canadian Northern Railway. By that date the two bustling centres had a combined population of 7,000, placing them second in urban size only to Sault Ste. Marie in all of Northern Ontario.

Elsewhere in Northwestern Ontario the last two decades of the 19th century witnessed the emergence of several other urban centres. Rat Portage, long a fur-trading post, was first incorporated as a Manitoba town in 1882. Ten years later it was re-incorporated, after the area was officially awarded to Ontario. In these years the community developed as a service centre for the surrounding Indian reserves, the lumber industry, and the Lake of the Woods gold mines, and in 1905 its name was changed to Kenora. Nearby Keewatin, favoured by a cheap water-power source and by its location on the CPR line, was the site of several sawmills and a large flour mill, erected in 1887. Eastward along the CPR main line, Ignace expanded as a railway divisional point and Dryden was established as an agricultural market community. That same role was played by Rainy River to the south, while Fort Frances was becoming a locally important commercial and lumbering village.

Sault Ste. Marie was the dominant urban centre in Northeastern Ontario in the late 19th century. The com-

munity was tied into the CPR network in 1887 with the completion of the Sudbury-Soo branch line, and into the American market with the construction of the International Railroad Bridge. That same year, by virtue of its population of 1,600, it gained the status of a town, and a minor real-estate boom involving the construction of new homes, schools, churches, and commercial buildings occurred. Urban amenities such as a fire brigade and sidewalks also appeared on the scene.

Even more dynamic for Sault Ste. Marie was the decade of the 1890s. The completion of the Canadian canal and lock system in 1895 and the entrepreneurship of Francis Hector Clergue brought about the industrial diversification of the town. New immigrant workers, many of them from Italy, settled in "Steelton" around the steel plant and swelled the population of Sault Ste. Marie from 2,400 in 1891 to 7,200 in 1901. They formed the nucleus of the Italian community that is still in existence today.

On Manitoulin Island during these years, lumbering, agriculture, and tourism combined to foster the growth of three small urban centres, Manitowaning, Gore Bay, and Little Current. Along the North Channel, established lumbering communities such as Blind River grew slowly in the 1890s, partly because of flagging markets and partly because of increased competition from new places such as Nairn and Webbwood.

As was the case in Northwestern Ontario, the construction of the CPR in the early 1880s completely altered the urban face of the northeast by creating several communities where none had been before. Sudbury, for example, was founded in 1883 as a CPR construction camp on the southern edge of the geological formation known as the Sudbury Basin. Thus it first functioned mainly as a railway centre and minor distribution point for the surrounding lumbering camps. Its future, however, was destined to be radically different. Copper and nickel, first discovered in the 1850s but then promptly forgotten, were rediscovered.

By the late 1880s small residential clusters, often consisting of little more than hastily constructed bunkhouses, had appeared at mine and smelter sites throughout the

8-10　*Disaster struck the Porcupine area in 1911,*
8-11　*when a bush fire destroyed the town and*
8-12　*killed 73 people (8-10). Golden Avenue in*
　　　South Porcupine was a tent row after the
　　　blaze (8-11), but by 1912 the wealth
　　　of the mines enabled the area to recover
　　　dramatically—buildings, boardwalks, and
　　　electric street lamps replaced the tents (8-12).

8-10

8-11

8-12

GOLDEN AVE. SOUTH PORCUPINE

8–13

8–14

8–15

8–16

Sudbury district, with Sudbury serving as their chief commercial focus. Incorporated as a town in 1893, Sudbury was to have greater difficulty in providing basic urban services than most northern communities, because of the lack of an industrial taxation base. In local contrast was Copper Cliff, the company-owned mining town dating from 1886, whose municipal services were provided by the Canadian Copper Company.

Even more of a creature of the CPR was North Bay, established in 1882 as a railway construction camp and divisional point. Its role as a transportation centre was enhanced in 1886 when the Grand Trunk Railway extended its line northward, first to Lake Nipissing and later to the CPR mainline. By the time the community was incorporated in 1891 it had acquired all the amenities associated with a town of 1,850 people, including a local newspaper. In the 1890s North Bay consolidated its position, although its population increased by only about 700.

From the turn of the century to the outbreak of World War I, the urban pattern of Northeastern Ontario changed considerably. The chief catalyst was the construction of the Temiskaming and Northern Ontario (T & NO) and National Transcontinental railways, which led to the discovery of new mineral deposits and the opening of new agricultural lands. Railway construction also created new villages and towns. The first important community founded as a result of the construction of the T & NO was Cobalt, a silver-mining town established in 1903. With its curved streets and haphazard building construction, it was the closest thing in Northern Ontario to the classical frontier "boomtown" mining community.

The boom at Cobalt in turn transformed nearby Haileybury, a farming village first established in the early 1890s and incorporated as a town in 1904, into the residential and commercial centre of the entire mining district. Prosperous mine owners built beautiful homes overlooking Lake Timiskaming, and thirsty miners fled "dry" Cobalt for the hotels of Haileybury. The third of the "Tri-towns," New Liskeard, was also fostered by these developments. A "farmer's town" situated on the south-ern fringe of the Little Clay Belt, it dated from the early 1890s and received its town charter in 1903.

The T & NO was also responsible for the creation of several smaller townsites along its route. Latchford, a point of departure for Gowganda and Elk Lake, was at first an important banking and hotel centre; since 1910, however, it has been a sawmilling community. Englehart was laid out in a geometric fashion befitting a divisional point on the railway. So too, when the first train pulled into Cochrane in 1908 it found a townsite drawn on a grand scale around Lake Commando, reflecting the popular view that the town would one day be the "metropolis of the north."

Between 1909 and 1911 the discovery of gold in the Porcupine district spawned seven separate townsites, including Golden City, Porcupine, South Porcupine, and Shuniah. A disastrous fire swept through the area in 1911, and out of the ashes a year later emerged the new town of Timmins. By World War I Timmins was a modern, bustling community, disproving the theory that mining camps could be little more than rough-and-ready frontier outposts. In the meantime the first traces of Kirkland Lake, another gold-mining town that was an outgrowth of earlier activity in Larder Lake and Swastika, appeared in 1911. Kirkland Lake's development as an urban centre, however, occurred after the Great War.

Of the older communities in Northeastern Ontario, North Bay benefited the most from these developments in the pre-war years. Its role as a transportation and communications centre was strengthened with the expansion of its northern hinterland, and between 1901 and 1911 its population tripled. For Sudbury and Sault Ste. Marie, growth was much more modest. The latter became a city in 1912, but only after a decade of fluctuating fortunes that had begun with the collapse of the Clergue steel empire in 1903.

In contrast, the Lakehead communities surged ahead, their combined populations increasing fourfold from 7,000 in 1901 to nearly 28,000 in 1911. In 1907 both Port Arthur and Fort William received city charters. Three of the largest grain elevators on the North American continent were built during this period, and the economic base of the twin cities was diversified with the addition of a giant lumber mill, a dry-dock and shipbuilding facility, a railway-car operation, and a flour mill. Symbolizing all of this development in 1913 was the construction of the Lakehead's first skyscraper, the eight-storey Whalen building in Port Arthur.

During the Great War a distinctive new feature—the comprehensively planned company town—was added to the urban picture in Northern Ontario. The first of these was Iroquois Falls, which was established in 1915 as a closed townsite by the Abitibi Power and Paper Company. Abitibi's plan included varied street patterns, zoning, and the creative use of open space. Several years later the company incorporated many of these innovations at another townsite, Smooth Rock Falls.

Kapuskasing, an Indian word meaning "divided waters," was the name given in 1917 to a location originally called McPherson. It also was a planned community, but in this case the planner was the government of Ontario, which hoped to avoid the formation of another closed company town in the north. Provincial authorities used the zoning principle to divide the townsite into four major land-use categories: business, industrial, residential, and greenbelt. Within the residential districts, provision was made to differentiate housing according to economic status, a feature later incorporated in other resource towns. In Kapuskasing, as in several other planned communities, there was a tendency for the townsite proper to be anglophone and the surrounding peripheries francophone in character.

In the urban history of Northern Ontario the inter-war years were unique, consisting of the roaring twenties and the depressed thirties, but they were also important because it was then that cities of a significant size appeared on the scene. The population of Timmins, for example, increased sevenfold from 3,800 in 1921 to 29,000 in 1941, making it the largest incorporated town in Canada. Another 10,000 people lived in the nearby towns of South Porcupine and Schumacher in 1941. The brightest

day in this period was undoubtedly January 31, 1934, when President Roosevelt of the United States raised the price of gold.

The other major urban centre to emerge in Northeastern Ontario was also a mining community, the "Nickel Capital of the World," Sudbury. Until World War I its population had been restricted by the fact that most workers lived at mine and smelter sites in communities such as Copper Cliff, Creighton, Coniston, and Levack. With the advent of the Sudbury–Copper Cliff streetcar system in 1915 and the flood of automobiles into the region in the 1920s, however, the mining workforce gradually shifted to Sudbury, and its population doubled to 18,000. This, combined with the increasing commercial and financial importance of the region, led to its incorporation as a city in 1930. Except for the first few extremely difficult years of the 1930s, when the mining industry collapsed, Sudbury escaped the worst effects of the Great Depression. By the middle of the decade both International Nickel and Falconbridge were expanding production and hiring workers at a rate unmatched elsewhere in Canada. Consequently, with a population of 32,000 in 1941, Sudbury had forged ahead of its other mid-north urban rivals.

Two of those rivals, North Bay and Sault Ste. Marie, grew only marginally in the inter-war period. North Bay, which acquired city status in 1925, was strengthened in its role as "Gateway to the North" with the completion of the Ferguson Highway north to Matheson in 1927 and the North Bay–Temiskaming Highway ten years later. In the mid-1930s the city enjoyed the international acclaim brought by the birth of the Dionne quintuplets at neighbouring Callander. In 1941 its population approached 16,000. By the same date Sault Ste. Marie had grown to 26,000 people, but that was an increase of only 5,000 from two decades earlier, reflecting the instability of the steel industry in these years.

In Northwestern Ontario both Fort William and Port Arthur grew steadily between the two wars; the population of the former increased from 21,000 to 31,000 and of the latter from 20,000 to 25,000 in this period. Both cities

8-17 *Often it was only through the efforts of individual community members that the smaller settlements gained the facilities and services they needed. The photograph behind William Foster is of Thornloe's children; the picture was taken to prove to the provincial government that a school was needed. The picture was sent, and the appeal succeeded. Gathered here with Mr. Foster are his wife Jean and daughter Mary Belle, during a pause in music making in 1917.*

8-18 *The arrival of the professional and entrepreneurial classes is an important part of urbanization; these groups provide essential services and often form an area's initial political organization. Byron Turner (centre) established a department store in Little Current in 1879. The firm is still in business, and Byron's descendants have been influential in local development and politics. This is a photograph of Turner's staff in 1905.*

8-19 *T.A. Austin's store in Chapleau on opening day, September 6, 1886. The building also housed a barber shop and post office; the Brotherhood of Locomotive Firemen met upstairs.*

8-17

8-18

8-19

8-20 *The construction of the town hall at Fort Frances, about 1905. Fort Frances had been incorporated as a village in 1903, after withdrawing from an earlier municipal organization that included surrounding townships. The new hall symbolized the community's growing awareness of itself as a political and economic unit.*

8-21 *The opening of the Port Arthur Electric Street Railway, 1892. The railway was built to connect Port Arthur with Fort William, where the CPR had concentrated its transshipment facilities the previous year.*

8-22 *The first grand jury of the Judicial District of Rainy River, posing in Fort Frances around 1908. Grand juries were empanelled for various reasons, for example, to discover whether a crime had been committed, or to examine conditions and make recommendations on roads, health care, or other public issues.*

8-20

8-21

8-22

insisted on maintaining their separate identities as an amalgamation vote was defeated in 1920. Both benefited from the pulp-and-paper boom in the region during the 1920s and suffered during the early years of the Depression. The opening of the Trans-Canada Highway in 1935 and the construction of a new airport in 1939 set the stage for the commercial recovery of the area, as well as promoting tourism. The World War II years accelerated the industrial diversification of both cities and reinforced their position as the dominant urban centres in the northwest. Other northwestern communities, such as Kenora, Fort Frances, Sioux Lookout, Dryden, and Rainy River, exhibited more modest growth patterns in these years.

In the decades following World War II several new planned resource communities were established throughout Northern Ontario. A typical community was Terrace Bay, the pulp-and-paper town that appeared on the north shore of Lake Superior in 1946. Its privately planned townsite included features such as the separation of residential and industrial sectors, the preservation and integration of the natural environment, the provision of an internal park system, and the creation of self-contained residential neighbourhoods. The townsite of Manitouwadge was drawn up by Government of Ontario planners, but it too displayed many of the characteristics found at Terrace Bay.

Manitouwadge in turn served as a model for Elliot Lake, the uranium-mining community established in 1956. Of all urban centres in Northern Ontario it came closest to being an instant city, as construction of the townsite was completed in only three years. By 1959 the first planning phase was essentially complete, and Elliot Lake had a population of nearly 25,000. The collapse of the American uranium market in the early 1960s dealt a devastating blow to the city, but since 1965 the need for nuclear-generated electrical power has gradually revitalized it. By the early 1980s urban expansion became necessary, and a second townsite incorporating many of the planning features of the first construction phase was added.

Northern Ontario's urban development in the post–World War II era has also been characterized by the emergence of a few dominant metropolitan centres. The growth of the largest of these, Sudbury, was tied closely during the 1950s and '60s to the nickel markets fostered by the Cold, Korean, and Vietnam wars. Falconbridge's expanded production at mines on the northern rim of the Sudbury Basin brought urban sprawl into the valley lowlands. This led to the enlargement of the city's boundaries in 1960 and then to the creation of the Regional Municipality of Sudbury in 1973. Within Sudbury itself, extensive suburbanization occurred to the northeast, as reflected in the construction of the New Sudbury Shopping Centre to serve the area in 1957.

The growth of suburbs such as New Sudbury caused the decline of downtown Sudbury as a shopping area. Consequently the late 1960s saw the undertaking of a major urban-renewal project that proved to be one of the most successful of its kind in Canada. A large section of the downtown core was completely transformed by the construction of a civic square housing city, regional, and provincial government offices; a shopping centre; a theatre; and several office, apartment, and housing complexes. Since 1978, too, the "greening of Sudbury," a land-reclamation program spearheaded by regional planning authorities and Laurentian University, has dramatically improved the appearance of the city and its environs.

While the decline of nickel-copper production and the introduction of new technologies in the mining industry brought about a population decrease in the Regional Municipality from 170,000 in 1971 to 160,000 in 1981, the Sudbury Basin will undoubtedly remain one of the world's leading mining and mineral-processing areas. As well, diversification of the local economy offers considerable promise for the future. Allied forms of industrial production, Sudbury's continuing role as Northeastern Ontario's chief commercial centre, the introduction of new tourist attractions such as Science North, and the existence of postsecondary institutions such as Cambrian

College and Laurentian University have combined to lessen the community's dependence on mining.

Since World War II Sault Ste. Marie has maintained its position as the second-largest city in Northeastern Ontario. A revitalized steel industry in the 1950s and '60s resulted in the expansion of civic boundaries through the annexation of Korah and Tarentorous townships. By 1971 its population had increased to more than 80,000, where it remains today. Sault Ste. Marie's cityscape has been revamped by the redevelopment of the downtown and waterfront districts, which was highlighted by the opening of Station Mall in 1973. The International Bridge and the Trans-Canada Highway have placed the city at the crossroads of a burgeoning tourist industry, and the presence of Algoma University College, an affiliate of Laurentian University, and the Northeastern Ontario regional offices of the Ministry of Northern Affairs have made it a major educational and government-service centre in the north.

In the post–World War II era North Bay continues to function as an important wholesale and retail distribution centre in the northeast. As well, a variety of secondary manufacturing operations, educational institutions such as Nipissing University College and Canadore College, a Canadian Forces Base, and a provincial mental-health facility have expanded the city's employment base. North Bay's location on Lake Nipissing has promoted tourism and fostered the establishment of numerous hotels and restaurants. In 1968 it annexed the neighbouring townships of Widdifield and West Ferris, doubling its population in the process. Since 1971 that population has remained at the 50,000 mark.

The fourth-largest urban centre in Northeastern Ontario, Timmins, failed to grow in the immediate postwar era, largely because of faltering gold markets and diminishing veins of economic ore. In the early 1960s the community gained a new lease on life with the opening of Kidd Creek Mines, and today copper mining is the city's economic backbone. Regional amalgamation in 1971 brought to Timmins both city status and the distinction of being the second-largest city (in area) in North America.

In Northwestern Ontario, Fort William and Port Arthur dominated the urban scene after World War II. Beneficiaries of the immediate postwar resurgence of Ontario's natural-resource sectors, both communities developed rapidly, their combined populations jumping from 65,000 in 1951 to 90,000 ten years later. The opening of the St. Lawrence Seaway in 1959 and the construction of the huge Keefer Terminal in 1962 carried the growth of the twin cities into the 1960s. In 1970 the long-discussed merger of Fort William and Port Arthur into a new entity, Thunder Bay, finally took place. The new city took pride in the province's reconstruction of Old Fort William on the banks of the Kaministikwia River beginning in 1971 and in the downtown redevelopment projects that centred on the Keskus and Victoriaville Malls. The success of these and other mall developments led to an expanded Inter-City Shopping Centre between the two former cities in 1982.

By 1981 Thunder Bay had become a major metropolitan centre, the most industrially diversified in Northern Ontario, supporting a population in excess of 121,000. It remains the world's largest grain-handling centre and is a pivot of the Canadian transportation system. Lakehead University and Confederation College make Thunder Bay the higher-education capital of the northwest. Served by three general hospitals and a psychiatric facility, it is also the chief health centre of the region. Finally, its scenic setting in the shadow of the "Sleeping Giant" and Mount McKay and its proximity to Kakabeka Falls ensure that tourism will continue to be important in the future.

8-23 *Port Arthur's water-supply intake pipe being lowered into Lake Superior, 3,500 ft. from shore, 1910. While schools and churches are obvious signs of urban growth, the less visible services such as sewers and water lines make urban life possible.*

8-24 *In 1944 the General Timber Co. built a pulp mill at Peninsula, near the mouth of the Pic River. The community grew rapidly, and within six months it was renamed Marathon. The rapid expansion of the town required the construction of a steel water tank, which towers over the wooden tank that serviced locomotives.*

8-25 *The Bruce Mines skating rink under construction, 1905, soon after the incorporation of the town. Bruce Mines is the oldest copper-mining community in Canada; the first permanent settlers were miners from the British Isles. When the mines closed in 1876, many residents stayed and turned to farming.*

8-23

8-24

8-25

8-26 *North Bay grew from uninhabited wilderness to city status in 43 years, being incorporated as a city in 1925. Its rapid growth was due to its position as a supply centre for lumbering and mining operations and good transportation systems. One of the signs of its growth was the replacement of wooden sidewalks with cement sidewalks in the 1920s.*

8-27 *Geraldton's first garbage-disposal wagon, 1936. It collected "garbage during the day and honey pots after dark."*

8-28 *Installing gas lines in Timmins, 1950s.*

8-29 *The Ontario Provincial Police were formed in 1909 to deal with labour-union strike activity in Northern Ontario's mining and lumber camps. This is the Timmins detachment, brought in during a strike.*

8-26

8-27

8-28

162

8-30 *Social services are among the last services provided to urban residents. In 1916 Cochrane's burned-out and homeless residents relied on voluntary donations of clothing at posts such as this one.*

8-31 *The staff of the Keewatin Hospital, undated. Left to right: Margit Oleson, Dr. Beatty, Miss Hanton, unknown, and Dr. Baker. The Keewatin-Kenora area is now served by a large central facility.*

8-32 *The delivery of proper health-care services in Northern Ontario has been difficult. Railway hospital cars and Red Cross outpost hospitals, staffed by Red Cross or public-health nurses, fulfilled an important need. Barbara Hincks (standing, left) served Matachewan in 1951. She taught prenatal classes as well as infant-care classes in the outpost hospital. Maternity cases were handled at home.*

8-33 *Ontario's air ambulances are an important part of the northern health-care system. Specially equipped aircraft, manned by attendants trained in skills needed in the northern climate, transport the critically ill or injured to hospitals in major cities, where specialized medical treatment is provided.*

8-29

8-30

8-31

8-32

8-33

8-34 *Urban renewal has changed the face of many*
8-35 *northern urban areas. In Sudbury's Borgia neighbourhood, renewal began in the late 1960s. 8-34, a 1967 view of Borgia from Mountain Street. It was then a working-class district. 8-35, Fournier Gardens, bottom centre, replaced much of the Borgia neighbourhood. This view also shows the new City Centre under construction in 1970.*

8-36 *The Sudbury Civic Square opened in 1977. This is a 1983 view.*

CHAPTER NINE

Culture and the Arts

JOAN KIVI-PIETILA
*Historical Researcher,
Thunder Bay.*

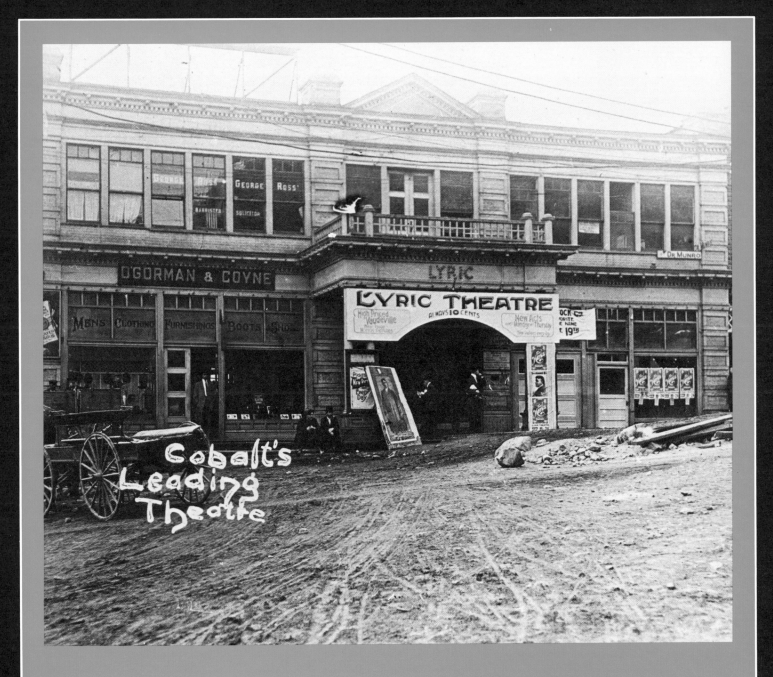

9–1 *Edifying, entertaining, educational, and
"always 10 cents," the high-calibre
vaudeville of Cobalt's leading theatre was
first-class recreation at the turn of the
century.*

9-2 The Indian drum ceremony was both a political and religious event, which helped integrate separate clan and family groups into a tribal community. This ceremony, commonly called a pow-wow, was held at Barwick, Rainy River, in 1899, for the benefit of the members of the legislative tour.

9-3 Protestant "revivalist" churches became common in the early 20th century. At first, tents were used for mobile camp meetings and in remote areas. This is the inside of a mission tent at Steelton, now part of Sault Ste. Marie, around 1910.

9-4 Education in small communities at the turn of the century depended on dedicated and often poorly paid staff. One-room schools sometimes accommodated children of all ages and from various ethnic backgrounds, so teachers had their hands full. 9-4, Howland No. 1 School in the 1920s. 9-5, a school in the North Bay area, about 1900.

9-2

9-3

9–4

9–5

9-6 *This orchestra of Finnish men practised and played at Nine Mile School, S.S. No. 4, McIntyre, near Port Arthur, in the early 1900s.*

9-7 *The Chapleau Brass Band was formed in 1888 and continues to the present day. This is the 1892 version of the band.*

9-6

9-7

Northern Ontario's culture is not limited to those people who frequent opera houses and art galleries. It includes the life of everyone, the ethnic groups and associations, who make up the population of Northern Ontario. The story of this land is one of architecture, religion, and education. When the basics of life have been achieved, people have turned to the enjoyment of music, dancing, theatre, the visual arts, and more recently, their own literature. Artistic expression in Northern Ontario has been dramatically affected by the close relationship artists feel to the land itself, and the experience of living in the north has inspired its residents to express its qualities in various media.

Two hundred years ago the culture of Northern Ontario was vastly different from what it is today. The area was inhabited by Cree and Ojibwa Indians and European traders and missionaries. Native men trapped, fished, hunted, and bartered with white traders to obtain the necessities of life, and the women spent much of their time looking after the needs of their husbands and children. However, they found time for beadwork, basketry, and jewelry making, and functional objects were often made beautiful through their skills. They also shared in smoking ceremonial tobacco, telling tales of the Thunderbird or the Windigo, and singing songs and dancing.

The fur traders at Michilimackinac, Sault Ste. Marie, Fort William, and Fort Frances enjoyed the music of the fiddle and the flute. Between 1803 and 1821, when Fort William was the main midsummer meeting place of the North West Company traders, the *Rendezvous* was a time of much singing, dancing, and drinking to distract the mind after months of work and hours of business meetings. Both the Great Hall frequented by the gentlemen and the *voyageurs'* encampment outside the palisade came to life during these days. After the union of the North West and the Hudson's Bay companies in 1821, this lively period came to an end.

Not until the 1880s and '90s did the north's culture change much. Then, with the discovery of new resources came new transportation systems and service centres. Towns sprang up, and their buildings showed almost as many architectural influences and styles as there were builders. Houses in the towns ranged from log cabins to pretentious homes built in the Georgian style. Entire communities were built of logs, as the bush camp reconstructed at Thunder Bay's Centennial Park demonstrates. In sharp contrast, the buildings at Dryden early in this century included only one log dwelling, the rest consisting of two-storey frame buildings erected in the space of a few weeks.

Although the Gothic Revival style might be seen in features such as the front windows, the houses generally lacked any distinctive style. Basically, architectural styles depended on the roles that particular buildings played. Banks and office buildings were often constructed in the Neoclassical style, and churches in the Gothic style made popular by early 19th-century romanticism.

The earliest forms of entertainment in these new towns involved activities within the family and neighbourhood circles. Leisure time was enriched by singing, playing instruments, dancing, and story-telling. Quilting bees were an opportunity for women to get together, and barn raisings became occasions for the whole community to work and socialize. Social life in the early years was encouraged by the establishment of Mechanics' Institutes, Young Men's and Young Women's Christian Associations, and Women's Institutes. Fraternal organizations such as the Masons and Knights of Columbus and various service clubs gave men occasion to meet. These associations organized clinics and libraries, as well as social events such as dances and movie or skit nights.

In time, cultural activities developed that involved the entire community. Schools played an important part in organizing elaborate Christmas concerts and huge picnics, especially in the spring. The whole community turned out to enjoy these events, especially the Christmas concerts, where children recited poetry, performed in plays, and sang carols. Churches were also important in the development of social and cultural activity, as persons of various denominations began to meet to share their beliefs.

Religion had long played an important part in the life of Northern Ontario. As new settlers arrived, homes, tents, and even barns served as the first locations for worship services, prayer meetings, and church socials. One of the earliest community activities in some cases was the erection of an appropriate church building. Christian services were at first organized by missionaries and ministers of the Roman Catholic, Anglican, Wesleyan Methodist, and Presbyterian "conservative" churches. Soon "revivalist" churches such as the Episcopal Methodists and Baptists began to appear. The ministers of both types of churches were often required to travel long distances on horseback or along the railway lines to minister to the faithful.

Education has always been a significant service in Northern Ontario. During the fur-trade era, many fathers sent their Métis children to Glengarry County in Upper Canada or even to Europe for a "European" education. In the settlement era, local efforts were again called for, as Ontario administrators were slow in providing for these needs. Initially children met in homes and churches, sometimes even in tents, to be taught. Eventually local school boards were created to meet these needs, and the first one- or two-room wooden school houses were built.

The success of these early educational efforts depended as much on enthusiasm as on training. The teachers rarely had much training, and salaries were too low to attract more than a few women to the profession. In spite of this the female teachers were quite successful in teaching the three R's and in encouraging children to enjoy music, art, drama, and creative writing.

The development of the educational system came to be largely in the hands of school inspectors such as W.J. Judd of Thunder Bay. An earlier inspector, J.E. MacDougall of North Bay, wrote *Building the North* in 1919, one of the first books on education in Northern Ontario. Children dreaded the recitations that the inspectors would require of them, and teachers dreaded the visits of these men even more, because their success in teaching their pupils was being rigorously tested.

Educating children in isolated communities required unique solutions in Northern Ontario. One solution was the use of school cars, adaptations of the most modern railway coaches of the time and well equipped as schools. The first cars set out in 1926, and eventually seven school cars operated along three different routes, the CPR main line, the CNR lines, and the T & NO railway line. They brought education to the families of railway workers, loggers, miners, trappers, fishermen, and hunters, both native and white, and from many ethnic backgrounds. These people welcomed the three- or four-day visits of the school cars. The cars represented a Canadianizing influence on the European settlers and ensured their allegiance to the Canadian government.

School cars provided cultural experience for the parents as well as education for the children. Part of the car had fifteen desks, even though there were often far more

9-9 Northern Ontario's turn-of-the-century settlers came from almost everywhere, and the buildings they constructed showed almost as many influences as there were builders. This is the Belair homestead on the Wolf River, Dorion, around 1919. The original building on the homestead was the saltbox, on the left. The new home on the right shows diverse influences.

9-10 A successful farmer in the Rainy River
9-11 valley and one of its pioneer homesteaders, Jimmy McOuat abandoned his agricultural lifestyle in 1898 to live on the Canadian Shield. He settled on the shore of the crystalline White Otter Lake, between Ignace and Atikokan. There he singlehandedly built the unusual log structure known as White Otter Castle and occupied it until his death in 1918. 9-10 shows the castle as it appeared during Jimmy's lifetime, with its four-storey tower and flower-filled front yard. In 9-11 Jimmy poses for a portrait to send to a prospective mail-order bride in 1887.

9-12 The Prairie school of architecture was represented at Kirkland Lake by the chateau that Sir Harry Oakes built there in 1919. The chateau was enlarged after a fire in 1929, and the interior has been renovated to house the Museum of Northern History.

9-8

9-9

9-10

9-11

9-12

9-13 *A Lakehead-area Baptist church choir, 1916. Churches provided an opportunity for everyone to express themselves in song; the more talented joined the choir or played the organ or piano. Many professional musicians began their careers by singing or playing instruments for their church.*

9-14 *Father Proulx in the Roman Catholic church at Chapleau, about 1900. The beauty of a church building was not necessarily an indication of a wealthy membership; often it was the sign of a dedicated congregation.*

children to be accommodated. The other part of the car provided living quarters for the teacher and his wife. During its visit the school car was the hub of activity in the community. People could expect practical help with their income tax returns and treats in the form of film presentations, bingo evenings, and parties. Even weddings and first communions are known to have taken place in the school cars.

The school car symbolized cultural development in Northern Ontario. Dedicated and well-trained teachers spent years travelling from place to place, bringing education and culture to isolated families. These teachers left the children with homework to complete before the car returned a few weeks later. Children learned to be highly independent as they learned reading, writing, and arithmetic, for the most part, on their own.

The end of the school-car system in 1967 did not end the development of unique educational methods in Northern Ontario. The Northern Corps, which had been created the preceding year, was a group of bright and energetic teachers devoted to the education of Ojibwa and Cree children in such remote places as Shining Tree, Gogama, Missanabie, and Ferland. Singly or in pairs, these teachers continue to bring educational challenges and cultural enrichment to these communities. The provision of schools in these areas has required much effort and expense. An unusual construction project initiated by R.R. Steele and J.A. Martin, Ministry of Education experts on northern schools, saw log-cabin schools built at Summer Beaver in 1977 and at Slate Falls the following year. Since the local residents built the schools, they are tailor-made to suit their needs.

Music has been a major form of cultural expression in Northern Ontario. Traditional folk songs, familiar to all the members of a community, were enjoyed by families and groups of friends. Often they sang to the accompaniment of pianos, fiddles, and other instruments. These songs found a larger audience in the 1940s, when folklore collectors began to "collect" folksongs.

Father Germain Lemieux, s.j., of Sudbury collected and published hundreds of Franco-Ontarian folktales and songs. He paid close attention to the material culture of these communities, looking at cooking, textile, and farming practices. A resource centre and museum presenting this material is being established in Sudbury.

Edith Fowke revealed the cultural life of the mining and lumbering camps by collecting English-language songs and stories of oldtimers. Joe Thibadeau sang her many songs of the Paul Bunyan days and told her tales of the Rainy River district. The "Lumberjack's Alphabet" is known wherever timber is cut. The "Porcupine Song" and the "Cobalt Song," the latter written by a young mining engineer named L.F. Steenman, are among the most widely known Canadian mining songs. They express the spirit and pride of the people who came to the early mining towns.

Choral groups, brass bands, string quartets, and orchestras were, and still are, popular in the towns. The Port Arthur Philharmonic Society, organized early in the century, had only a short life. The role of creative individuals has been recognized in New Liskeard, where the Ladies' Philharmonic Choir flourished before it was renamed the Ruby Dunn Watten Memorial Choir in 1941. This group has been awarded the highest award in Canadian choral music, the Lincoln trophy. New Liskeard music lovers also initiated the Temiskaming Festival of Music in 1958; this festival has ever since encouraged the enjoyment of music among the people of Northeastern Ontario.

Northern Ontario musicians have achieved a high level of excellence and national recognition. Sudbury's Trump (Jimmy) and Teddy Davidson were among the first to play jazz music in Canada. Starting in the mid-1920s and ending only recently, Trump played the cornet and Teddy played the tenor saxophone to appreciative audiences. Jeanne Pengelly, a soprano from Port Arthur, made her debut at the Metropolitan Opera in 1936 and had a distinguished career in Canadian music. The current popularity of francophone performers such as Cano and Robert Paquette comes in part from their blending of traditional and modern music.

9–13

9–14

9-15 *The most common entertainments in new settlements were the informal times at home. The traditional entertainments are still popular in the more isolated communities; these Fort Albany men are dancing in a kitchen to the music of a friend's harmonica in the 1940s.*

9-16 *The Loyal Orange Association was one of the many international organizations and service clubs that gave men in Northern Ontario occasion to meet and socialize regularly. These La Vallee members are celebrating the 217th anniversary of William of Orange's victory at the Battle of the Boyne on July 12, 1690.*

9-17 *The Women's Institute, one of the first organizations in Canada established specifically for the benefit of rural women, helped break down the isolation of the early settlers. It thrived in Northern Ontario. This is the Green Bay WI, meeting at the home of Mrs. L. W. Ferguson at Sheguiandah in 1908. The WI was introduced into Manitoulin Island in 1905, and by 1912 there were thirteen branches with a total of 235 members.*

9-15

9-16

9-17

9-18

The establishment of the symphony orchestras at Sudbury and at the Lakehead presented opportunities for Northern Ontario musicians and attracted others to the region. The Lakehead Symphony Orchestra engaged the Princeton String Quartet in 1969 to perform and conduct the Symphony School of Music. Under maestro Dwight Bennett, a symphony chorus has also been organized and a number of fully staged operas have been performed. In Sudbury, orchestra director Metro Kozak and his wife Mary head a thriving Suzuki violin teaching program that introduces even preschoolers to the joys and rigours of formal music training.

The music scene in Northern Ontario has also been enriched by ethnic choirs, bands, and dance groups. There are Scottish pipe bands, Croatian Tamburitza orchestras, and Ukrainian mandolin ensembles. The Kiikurit Finnish folk dancers of Thunder Bay and the Ukrainian Carpathian dancers from Sault Ste. Marie make a large contribution to dance in Northern Ontario.

At the beginning of the century, dances were the most popular form of entertainment in almost every community. Often the dances had specific themes, for example, neck-tie dances required each man to match a miniature tie pinned to his lapel with an identical tie hidden inside one of the lunch boxes held by the ladies. There were also hard-time dances, masquerade dances, and Christmas dances. A shortage of women did not discourage the pleasure of the dance party for the men in the lumber camps or survey crews. Sometimes men dressed themselves comically in dresses and hats to hold a stag dance.

The history of the theatre arts in Northern Ontario began with the travelling road shows that brought dramatic productions to the region. They performed plays and musicals in any available building, even in barns. Sudbury was fortunate, as early as 1902, to have a brick opera house that could stage any company that came to town. With the construction of the Grand Theatre in 1908, Sudbury gained the reputation of being a real show town.

Even smaller towns could enjoy the Chautauqua, a series of shows that travelled from town to town to amuse and educate people. Other activities, even work in some places, were set aside when the Chautauqua company arrived, pitched its giant tents, and presented a program of speakers, musicians, dancers, and actors. Even the movie houses had to yield to the Chautauqua when it arrived to present its summer show.

The theatre life of Northern Ontario was deeply affected by the motion picture industry. Movie theatres sprang up all across the region to present the latest Hollywood movies as well as vaudeville and novelty acts. The latter included women of superhuman strength and other women who floated around the theatre in giant balloons. Although early motion pictures were silent, a pianist would accompany the action or a child might earn a nickel pumping the player piano. "Talkies" appeared at the beginning of the 1930s. In those lean times, whoever could afford the required dime paid it willingly to get into the theatre and enjoy the newsreels, movies, and musicals that came to life before them.

The appearance of television in the 1950s threatened the popularity of both movies and live theatre, but there are always people who enjoy performing and others who appreciate live performances. As a result Northern Ontario now has a number of accomplished professional and amateur theatre groups. Sudbury has a full-time professional theatre company, the Sudbury Theatre Centre. In North Bay the Theatre and Arts Community Centre is the focal point for all the performing arts, including the resident professional company, the Theatre Circle. In Thunder Bay, Magnus Theatre produces professional performances, and there is also an array of active amateur groups.

The visual arts have produced many dramatic developments through the years. The Northern Ontario art record goes back about five hundred years to the Cree and Ojibwa pictographs. The artists, using paints made from the earth and their fingers as brushes, captured the realities of their lives on rock faces along the northeastern shores of Lake Superior, in Nipigon country and Quetico Park, and in the Lake of the Woods region. Selwyn Dewdney and Kenneth E. Kidd brought this art to a wider audience in the 1960s with photographs and drawings of these natural galleries.

Northern Ontario's visual arts did not receive a similarly dramatic expression until Tom Thomson began to paint the beauties of Georgian Bay and the near north early in this century. Thomson's paintings attracted the attention of a group of Toronto-based painters who in 1920 became the Group of Seven. Their paintings of the Northern Ontario landscape, inspired by the lonely vistas, windswept forests, and frozen lands, radically altered the Canadian art scene. Their paintings and the atmosphere they evoked came to seem so unmistakably Canadian that their work could be called the National Style.

The new development of native people's painting has found an international clientele. Norval Morrisseau's work of the 1960s caught the eye of art lovers across the country and led other talented natives of Northern Ontario to express themsleves in painting. The "Woodland School" in the 1960s included Carl Ray, Daphne Odjig, and Goyce and Joshim Kakegamic. In recent years, artists at Sandy Lake and the James Bay communities have captured on canvas aspects of their mythical past and of their present culture and philosophy of life.

Native artists often focus on warm family relationships and deep kinship with nature in their paintings. They capture the spiritual qualities of plants, animals, and human beings through imaginative symbols and rich colours. They sometimes work together through groups such as the Triple K Co-operative, organized at Red Lake in 1973. Another company of seven artists began in 1977 among the Cree from the James Bay area. The Weneebaykook Co-operative creates silkscreen prints in limited numbers, using each artist's unique style and favourite themes to convey their message.

The importance of these paintings was highlighted in 1982, when the Centre for Indian Art was established as an addition to the Thunder Bay National Exhibition Centre. The two centres serve the aesthetic needs of northerners by exhibiting paintings and other art forms in their spacious galleries as well as providing a focal point for the historical research, collection, and documentation of art.

Folk art in Northern Ontario includes the work of various European immigrant artists, as well as that of British and French Canadians and natives. The Native Arts and Crafts Corporation designs, produces, and distributes the work of talented artists in the Thunder Bay region. Jonas Mockas, who is Lithuanian-born, does intricate wood carvings; Frank Potocnik, born in Slovenia, is famous for his sculpture; and Yugoslavian-born Paul Molnar has exhibited his paintings in Toronto and New York. Wikwemikong painter and carver Angus Trudeau fills large canvases with portrayals of Great Lakes steamers; these hang in the National Gallery as well as in his store.

The literature of Northern Ontario has developed more slowly than the visual arts have. At the turn of the century, most authors who wrote about the region were not residents. While living in Toronto, Alan Sullivan wrote *The Rapids* (1920), which immortalized Francis H. Clergue's endeavours at Sault Ste. Marie. There were some significant Northern Ontario writers, however, such as the Iroquois poet, Pauline Johnson, who wrote in Fort William in the 1890s.

Recently natives have taken up the collecting and publishing of Indian stories. In 1974 Norval Morrisseau revealed story-telling ability in addition to his artistic skill with *Legends of My People, The Great Ojibway*. Non-native literature has also developed; regional publishers, notably the Highway Book Shop in Cobalt and Penumbra Press in Moonbeam, have published books by Northern Ontario authors. Many of these deal with the history of the region and explore the culture of Northern Ontario.

An interesting development among writers in several communities is the organization of groups whose members encourage each other to write as well as criticize the work. Such groups include the Lake of the Woods Group in Kenora and the Dryden Writers' Group, which organized the 1983 Squatchberry Festival, an annual weekend of readings, workshops, and social events. Many Northern Ontario authors contribute to the *Squatchberry Journal*, edited and published in Geraldton by Edgar Lavoie. The journal features writers and artists who deal with North-

9-19 *A Chinese float in a parade in Port Arthur,
probably in the 1930s. Fraternal and
ethnic organizations and clubs provided
entertainment and recreation for their
members, and parades offered all members of
the community an opportunity to either
participate or observe.*

ern Ontario themes, in prose—both fiction and nonfiction—and in poetry.

Journalists have also made major contributions to the north's literature. Newspapers not only publish the news; they provide a forum for community opinion and help to create the community's sense of identity. One of the pioneers was W.D. Smith, founding editor of the *Manitoulin Expositor* in 1879, who wrote, set type, printed, and distributed the newspaper himself. The *Expositor* remains the oldest privately owned newspaper in Northern Ontario. In 1983 it won the Michener Award for meritorious public service.

Northern Ontario's two universities have also encouraged the growth of a regional culture. Laurentian University's many contributions include the bilingual *Laurentian University Review*. Lakehead University's faculty members have chartered aircraft and rented cars to take university courses to the scattered communities of Northwestern Ontario.

In recent years, cultural and artistic development has been promoted by radio and television stations, museums and art galleries, and newspapers and journals. Regional organizations have emerged to encourage the use of northern content and to develop a sense of unity in Northern Ontario. They have been assisted by federal and provincial government agencies, who recognize that the Northern Ontario cultural mosaic makes a substantial contribution to Canadian culture.

9-19

9-20 *One solution to the problem of supplying*
9-21 *educational facilities in remote communities was the institution of the school-car system. The first cars set out in 1926, and eventually seven cars operated along the CPR, CNR, and T & NO lines. Part of each car had fifteen desks, even though there were often far more children to be accommodated. The other part of the car provided living quarters for the teacher and his wife. During its three or four-day visit the school car was the hub*

of activity in the community; there were film presentations and bingo nights, and even weddings sometimes took place in the school cars. The system operated until 1967.

9-20

9-21

9-22 Teacher and folklorist Père Germain Lemieux, s.j., launches his hand-built model of a Canadian Corvette for a group of children from the Flour Mill district of Sudbury, 1952. The sale of the boat raised funds for the collection of French Canadian folklore material.

9-23 Schools played an important part in encouraging interest in the theatre arts. These budding actresses performed in a Fort Frances high school, perhaps in the 1930s.

9-24 Members of Le Centre des Jeunes-Civitas Christi de Sudbury, singing in the St. Jean Baptiste Day Parade in 1953. The centre, founded by Father Albert Regimbal, s.j. and Jacques Groulx in 1950, is now the largest French cultural centre in Ontario.

9-25 These children's versions of traditional costumes and uniforms mark their membership in the Polish community, both for themselves and their audience.

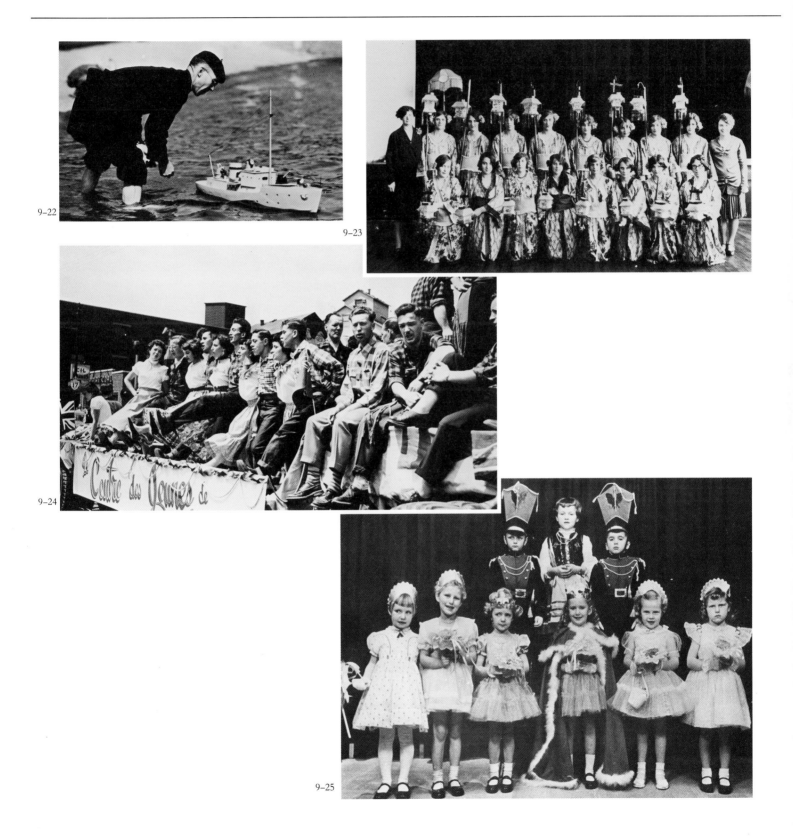

9-22

9-23

9-24

9-25

9-26 *The Croatian Tamburitza Orchestra at the Croatian Home in Port Arthur, late 1930s.*

9-27 *Mavis Hewitt performed in this dance outfit at Fort William's Orpheum Theatre during a recital by Grace Ensworth, her instructor, in 1925.*

9-28 *Most towns in Northern Ontario had a theatre or opera house by the 1920s, although even before this travelling road shows performed plays and musicals in any available building, even barns. Vaudeville acts were always popular; this amateur group is the Silver Town Minstrels, photographed in Cobalt in 1926. The rise of the motion-picture industry rang the death knell for most of these acts.*

9-26

9-27

9-28

9–29 *Norval Morrisseau demonstrates the techniques of his art to an appreciative group of students. Born in Fort William in 1932, Morrisseau was raised on the Sandy Point Reserve on Lake Nipigon. While he was working as a miner, a vision instructed him to depict the legends of his people, the Ojibwa. He obtained art supplies from Selwyn Dewdney, who had been instrumental in making the Canadian public aware of Northern Ontario's pictographs.*

His first public showing in Toronto in 1962 was a tremendous success, and since then his work has influenced a whole generation of native artists.

9–30 *Painter Ivan Wheale relaxes in his studio at Sheguiandah, 1984.*

9–31 *Religious and artistic expression are combined in the icons of St. Mary's Church in Sudbury, here being painted in 1954.*

9–32 *A quilting workshop in West Bay, 1983. Rose Peletier, Elizabeth Ense, and Maimie Migwans practice a craft that was once more of a "survival skill" and a very important part of social life for women in rural communities.*

9–29

9–30

9–31

9–32

9-33 *Kathrene Pinkerton, author of* Wilderness Wife, *with Col. D. F. Young of Quetico Forest Reserve standing behind her, about 1912 at Eva Lake.*

9-34 *The Cockburn Theatre in Sturgeon Falls, 1930s. With the arrival of the motion picture, even those in isolated communities could enjoy the movies, newsreels, and musicals that before had been available only in larger urban centres to the south. At times movie theatres presented plays and vaudeville and novelty acts as well.*

9-35 *The itinerant opera company has been replaced by the mail-order movie in many communities. Here a Department of Lands and Forests officer shows conservation movies to the residents of Ogoki in 1955.*

9-33

9-34

9-35

CHAPTER TEN

Sports and Recreation

JOE GREAVES
Curator, Northwestern Ontario Sports Hall of Fame,
Thunder Bay.

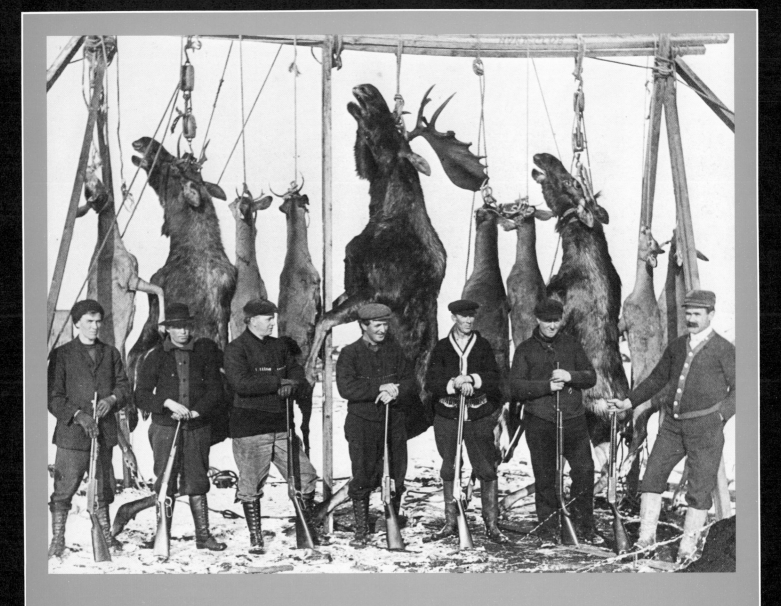

10-1 *This party hunted in the McGregor Bay area and were photographed with their kill on Spider Island in 1911. Big-game hunting, once a survival skill, had by this time become a sport for most hunters. In the future, visiting hunters would provide a major source of revenue for some Northern Ontario communities.*

10-2 *Jack DiGiacomo of Fort William won bicycle-racing trophies at Winnipeg and Lakehead meets in the 1930s.*

10-3 *A snowshoe outing near Cochrane in the 1920s.*

10-2

10-3

10-4 *The Sunrise Bombers baseball team was sponsored by the Sioux Lookout Bakery in the 1930s.*

10-5 *The McKenzie Island baseball team, about 1943. By this time, intercommunity and industrial leagues were common in Northern Ontario. Corporate support for baseball and hockey had increased during the Depression; employers hired skilled players and allowed them flexible work schedules to enable them to play. The men were given employment, and the community was provided with entertainment.*

10-4

10-5

10-6 Boxing's popularity increased after World
War I, when its benefits for both physical
training and entertainment became obvious.
These lumbercamp workers are obviously
more interested in the entertainment side of
things. This match took place at Camp 10
of the D. A. Clark Co. near Nipigon in
1936. The crowd is roped off, a pail of water
is handy for reviving, and a handbell marks
the rounds.

10-7 The Chapleau YMCA Physical Club,
1916. The early 20th century was a period
of rapid growth for the YMCAs and
YWCAs in Northern Ontario. Encouraged
by the churches, these clubs provided an
opportunity for young men and women to
increase their "health, strength, and purity."

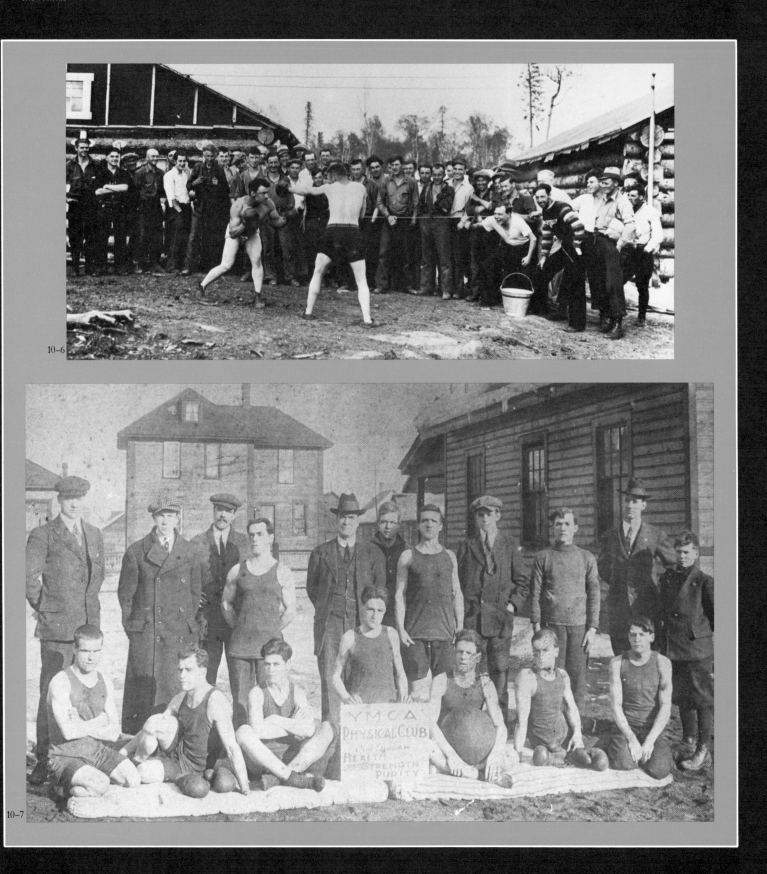

10-6

10-7

R

ECREATIONAL ACTIVITIES have long been important to the residents of Northern Ontario. The environment is suited to the enjoyment of a wide range of outdoor recreational activities, some of them only a little removed from the original occupations of the native people. Fishing and hunting, canoeing and camping now provide a necessary antidote to the demands of contemporary occupations. Providing facilities for these activities, including the maintenance of provincial parks and preserves, has become a full-time occupation for many Northern Ontarians.

The enjoyment of sports as a form of recreation has developed within the past one hundred years. One of the curiosities of this development is the tension between sports in which a few persons are players and many more enjoy the game as spectators, and recreational sports activities in which many people are participants. Growing participation in recreational activities during the past quarter-century has shifted attention away from the major sports of earlier days and reduced the level of play that local spectators can enjoy.

One of the first sports to be played in Northern Ontario was lacrosse, which originated among the native peoples of North America. It was enthusiastically taken up by new residents in the 1890s, with young men playing the game in and for various towns. In 1901 the New Ontario Lacrosse Association was formed in Northeastern Ontario. Within five years, however, the popularity of the game had peaked, and lacrosse was abandoned by people who found baseball a far more interesting summer sport. Several attempts to re-establish lacrosse during the next half century did not succeed, although it has been making a comeback in the past decade.

Baseball first began to be played in the United States in the 1860s and aroused some interest in the towns of Northern Ontario as they grew in the 1890s. In the early years the game was played on an amateur and periodic basis; civic holidays and community events presented opportunities for teams to be formed on diamonds that were often far cruder than today's ball parks.

Churches were a major influence on the development of sport in the late 19th century. In the period that saw rapid growth of the Young Men's and Women's Christian Associations, churches recognized the importance of exercise and encouraged various forms of sport as acceptable recreation for their members. Church young people's groups found accommodation in church basements or specially constructed halls for such sports as badminton. Church property sometimes provided space to construct tennis courts for use by members of the congregation and their friends.

Gymnastic and track clubs were also inspired by the early churches, especially the Lutheran churches that served Finnish immigrants. In many cases, these sports clubs were developed by churches to stimulate community interest in these churches and to hold the congregation together. Similar motives led to the establishment of church-sponsored canoe clubs, out of which grew some of the country's best-known rowing clubs, as well as baseball and hockey teams.

The introduction of sports has often been related to the social composition of a community, especially the ethnic origins of its residents. Thus the Scottish game of curling was taken up by the business and professional men of Northern Ontario at the beginning of the 1890s. No game has proved more captivating over the years for people of all ages and both sexes. Bill Tetley, the Canadian Brier winner in 1975, has competed with his mother at lead, his son second, and his wife third. Every town in Northern Ontario enjoys its own curling club, with buildings that have usually been built and maintained by members of the club. The focus has usually been on club or social curling, with only a few rinks aspiring to national and world competition.

Hockey joined baseball and curling as popular sports in the late 19th century. Each of these games gave players a chance to display individual prowess in a team context and encouraged rivalries between towns, as teams were invested with the prestige of the communities they represented. Games between such teams became the most popular form of entertainment during the first half of this century, as whole communities turned out to support their home teams. In the small railway and mining towns of Northern Ontario, where many of the residents were recent European immigrants working hard as railway workers, miners, pulpwood cutters, and teamsters, few had time to play Canadian games, and they found them quite unfamiliar. Loyalty to the home team was not alien, however, and they loved the competition between their team and teams from other towns. Sports thus assisted the naturalization process of these new Canadians.

Only very late did municipal authorities or the provincial government assist by providing sports facilities. In the early years local initiative provided the ice surfaces required for that most popular of winter games, hockey. The first rink at the Lakehead was established on common ground used in the summer for grazing cattle. The area was cleared and levelled and then flooded. Boards were placed around the intended ice surface and water drawn from a well or the Kaministikwia River. Two days of work and 140 barrels of water were required to produce the rink. As early as 1887, an attempt was made at the Lakehead to construct a covered rink. The roof was made of canvas kept suspended by ropes attached to poles at the edge of the rink. As snow accumulated, however, the canvas would begin to sag, and eventually the sagging centre prevented players from seeing the other end of the rink. One imaginative solution to this problem was to attach the supporting ropes to pulleys so that the roof could be lowered before, and raised again after, each snow storm.

It was in these ways that hockey became Canada's national sport. It was a game that could be played by children and adults at their various levels of skill. Outdoor rinks, including frozen ponds, dotted every community. The vacant lot down the street became a gathering spot for the children, as the sheet of ice provided winter fun for them. Fancy equipment was hardly necessary, although a pair of skates and a hockey stick were required. A couple of magazines thrust beneath his stockings then equipped the boy to play hockey with the best of them. Northern Ontario towns became training grounds for hockey players in much the same way that the southern United States produced baseball players. The neighbourhood rink held the boy's attention without adult supervision for hours on end. The shinny he played made him a stickhandler rarely matched in later years. Some of the best players began playing in these simple surroundings of unorganized recreation.

The growth of team sports during the 1910s and '20s resulted in the organization of leagues in the eastern parts of Northern Ontario. A North Shore Baseball League, including teams of professional players based in Sudbury, Copper Cliff, Webbwood, and Massey, was organized in 1908 and recruited players from as far away as New York state. This effort hardly survived the first season, except in Copper Cliff, where the International Nickel Company helped to support the team. A more permanent

10-8 *The camp cook and photographer with his helper at the Wabinosh Cache camp near Nipigon, 1910. Although the cook probably regarded his picture-taking as recreation, it had a much larger significance. Photographs often provided the first records of settlement in Northern Ontario in the late 19th and early 20th centuries. Without the amateur photographer, this book wouldn't have been possible.*

10-9 *Not all forms of competition and recreation are sports. The fall fair at New Liskeard in 1903 was an opportunity for participants to test and compare skills in the domestic, horticultural, and agricultural arts.*

10-10 *The Sturgeon Falls poolroom in the 1920s was an academy of the manly arts of billiards and cigar smoking. Some say proficiency in billiards is the sign of a misspent youth, but* today there are prestigious and financially rewarding world-class tournaments for the skilled pool player.

10-11 *Surveyors in the Temiskaming District, 1920s, engaging in what is probably the most common form of recreation: a little talk, a little smoke, a bit of music, and lots of laughs.*

10-8

10-9

10-10

10-11

10-12 *A North Bay field lacrosse team and its mascot, around 1910. Lacrosse developed from a North American Indian game, Baggataway, which was played with a stick similar to a bishop's crozier (la crosse). Teams from a number of Northern Ontario towns competed in the 1890s and early 1900s, but by the time this picture was taken, lacrosse's popularity was on the wane.*

10-13 *North Shore and Manitoulin hockey leagues were organized around 1890 for both men and women. Teams travelled, usually in the covered mail-sleigh, from Killarney to Little Current, Little Current to Gore Bay, and from there to towns along the North Shore. This women's team played for Gore Bay, probably around 1910.*

10-14 *As lacrosse declined in importance, baseball's popularity grew. By the time this picture of the Emo ball team was taken, probably before World War I, baseball had become the summer team sport.*

10-15 *Few sports in Northern Ontario have been as captivating for all ages and both sexes as curling has been. This is the Dome Mines Ladies' Curling Rink of Timmins in 1943, the year it won the Northern Ladies' Curling Association championship.*

190

10-16 *Then as now, baseball was enthusiastically taken up by women as well as men. This team played in Dryden.*

10-17 *Jim Espaniel of Biscotasing, posing with all the equipment needed to play hockey in 1925. Espaniel became the chief of a Biscotasing band and was a friend of Archie Belaney (Grey Owl).*

organization was achieved in 1913 with the Nickel Belt Baseball League, which included teams from Sudbury, Copper Cliff, and Creighton. Even in these early years, teams were sometimes strengthened by tempting a good player to one of the communities with a promise of employment in the mines or smelter.

The development of hockey leagues followed a similar course. Efforts to establish an International Hockey League in 1912 and the New Ontario Hockey League were short-lived. Not until 1919 was the Northern Ontario Hockey League organized, with teams from North Bay, Sault Ste. Marie, Sudbury, Cobalt, and New Liskeard included in it. The Sudbury team topped a fine season to win the Allan Cup in 1920 and launched the illustrious history of the Sudbury Wolves. The Nickel Belt Hockey League appeared in 1926.

Although the play in Northern Ontario was lively, only rarely would it come to the attention of Toronto or Montreal sports writers. Canadians were astonished in 1907, when a Rat Portage hockey team challenged the powerful Montreal Wanderers to play for the Stanley Cup and then defeated them. The victory was a source of great local pride. The town of Rat Portage renamed itself Kenora, and the fame of the Kenora Thistles was established for all time.

Local pride did not keep able players in their home towns for very long. The opportunity to play professionally in a big-city team drew many players out of Northern Ontario. This became particularly clear in the mid-1920s, when the National Hockey League (NHL) was being organized and whole teams were recruited from senior amateur ranks. The Port Arthur Tricolours were one of the best senior teams of that era, winning the Allan Cup in the 1924-25 and 1925-26 seasons and again in 1928-29. This team lost more than a dozen of its stars to the NHL.

Corporate support for teams received a remarkable impetus during the 1930s. The ability to play baseball or hockey could be parlayed into employment and a steady income for young men who might otherwise have been in the relief camps. Industrialists, concerned about the welfare of their community, saw the possibilities of supporting baseball and hockey teams as a way to encourage community feeling and provide entertainment. Managers were encouraged to hire skilled players and to allow them the flexible work schedules that full participation in sports required. Company executives were frequently at the head of sports organizations to indicate their support for the team. This policy was never more evident than in the Sudbury area, where the Nickel Belt baseball and hockey leagues flourished during this period.

Competition in baseball and hockey was very keen among the mining and smelting centres of Coniston, Copper Cliff, Creighton, Falconbridge, and Frood. The Nickel Belt leagues attracted some of the best athletes in the country because of the work to be obtained in the mines. The Nickel Belt Baseball League bordered on semi-professional status, as players from all parts of Canada made their way to Sudbury in search of baseball jobs. One of the most famous was Phil Marchildon of Penetanguishene, who had several successful seasons in the Nickel Belt, then obtained a tryout in the American major leagues and achieved an impressive pitching record with Connie Mack's Philadelphia Athletics.

The Lakehead communities were among the biggest suppliers of athletes to the Nickel Belt hockey and baseball leagues. At one time, no fewer than eleven Lakehead players played on the Creighton Mine hockey team. Some of the best baseball players in the port cities, including Guy Perciante and Weikko Koivisto, made their way to the mines to work and play for money. The funds available for sport were evident in the fact that Copper Cliff had a hockey arena complete with artificial ice by 1935, an unusual achievement for a small centre.

Hockey flourished in Northern Ontario during the Great Depression. Established mining communities outside the Nickel Belt produced contenders for the Northern Ontario Hockey Association championship, and the "old" centre of Sault Ste. Marie produced teams that were not to be ignored. The new gold mines at Geraldton and Longlac also sponsored hockey teams, with the Geraldton Goldminers producing impressive results. The greatest achievements were those of Sudbury Basin teams, including the Sudbury Cub Wolves, who won the Memorial Cup in 1932; the Frood Mine Tigers, who won the Allan Cup in 1937 and went on to win the world tournament in Toronto that spring; and the Sudbury Wolves team that Max Silverman took to Europe in 1938 to win the world championship in Prague.

The 1930s were years of sports achievement in other ways as well. The influences were quite diverse, as indicated by the fact that the Sudbury Canoe Club sponsored women's baseball and hockey teams and helped to begin the era of broader participation in sports. Among the other achievements in this era at Sudbury were the first winning figure skaters, who developed their art within the Copper Cliff Skating Club, and several speed skaters. These individual accomplishments were matched by the growing popularity of skiing, which had been introduced into Northern Ontario much earlier by Finnish and Scandinavian immigrants. It remained largely an ethnic sport for several decades, but in these years others became interested in skiing, and clubs such as the Algonquin Ski Club were established to find a suitable hill and purchase it, if they had to, or just use it if it were not clearly private property. To develop the ski hills and modest jumps of these first ski areas required much physical labour, which the members supplied, and some heavy equipment, which local companies were often happy to lend. The funds needed were raised by various methods, including bond issues to the public.

The resourcefulness of Northern Ontario can be appreciated today at the Northwestern Ontario Sports Hall of Fame, where the displays include skates hammered out of steel files, and home-made skis and curling stones. The ingenuity these crude artifacts reveal was also expressed in other equipment improvements in Northern Ontario. At the beginning of the 1920s skates were constructed with the heel and toe plate in line and parallel to the ice. The skate sharpener for the Port Arthur Tricolours in 1924 was Louis Sprovieri, an Italian shoemaker who had become an ardent hockey fan. His knowledge of shoemaking and skating led him to design a special heel for hockey boots, which he offered to his players and sold

to others. The innovation having proved quite successful, Sprovieri applied for a patent and attempted to obtain financial recognition from makers of hockey boots who were incorporating the "Sprovieri Heel." His legal struggle to obtain a fee for commercial production of these boots failed, however, as skate manufacturers raised the heel strut above the level of the toe strut, giving skates the rockered effect that made sharp turns easier and improved manoeuvrability in general.

Another equipment innovation developed out of the needs of Edgar Laprade, a small but outstanding stickhandler with the New York Rangers, who found his opponents endlessly slashing at his ankles as they sought to relieve him of the puck. He had heavy leather tendon protectors sewn onto his skates and, as this improvement was adopted by other players, manufacturers began to include tendon guards as a regular feature of high-quality skates.

Still another equipment advance of the interwar years developed within the industrial capacity of the Lakehead. The timing of hockey games, including penalties, had long depended on individual timekeepers and their stopwatches. It was easy for the timekeeper to be a few seconds off in measuring penalties or ending period plays, sometimes with regrettable consequences. A Lakehead jeweller had struggled for years with the idea of a timepiece that would give officials, players, and spectators a clear idea of how the game was progressing. After nearly twenty years of experimenting, J.W. Martin enlisted the assistance of a friend, Fenton Ross, who worked at the Port Arthur Shipbuilding Company. They perfected the Sportimer, a giant clock that told the time played, the minutes of penalties, and the score, all under the control of switches in the timekeeper's box at rink level. The Port Arthur Shipbuilding Company produced this revolutionary device for Maple Leaf Gardens and the Montreal Forum, as well as Northern Ontario rinks. The drawings for a custom-made Toronto clock, completed in 1929, reveal a Sportimer that was five feet square, with four faces, a minute hand in black and a second hand in red, and letters that were four inches high. The inventors

10-18 *Hockey is still played in the streets, with or without ice. This game of scrub hockey was played at Bearskin Lake. With 45-gallon drums marking the net, it was probably easy to hit the post with a shot on goal.*

10-19 *Edgar Laprade, here shown in 1939, contributed to the development of tendon guards. He had heavy leather protectors sewn onto his boots to protect him from* slashing sticks. *This improvement was adopted by other players, and later manufacturers began to include it as a regular feature of high-quality skates.*

10-20 *Without the amateur hockey associations that support the midget, juvenile, and junior leagues, young players would have no opportunity to develop the skills they need to become major-league players. This is the* Keewatin Junior Hockey Team and their trophy in 1937.

10-21 *The Kenora Rowing Club in the 1920s.*

10-22 *Soccer was and still is most popular with European immigrants, both from Britain and the continent. The La Vallee soccer team was organized at the turn of the century.*

10-18

10-19

10-20

10-21

10-22

10-23 *The New Liskeard Alerts athletic team was organized in 1932. One team member, Mary Vanderfleet (Graydon) (fifth from left), competed in the 100-yard races and relay at the 1932 Los Angeles Olympic Games. The Alerts competed in the British Empire Games and the Canada Games in Halifax.*

10-24 *Scandinavians and Finns introduced and popularized gymnastics in Northern Ontario. Field gymnastics was a blend of acrobatics, dance, and displays of suppleness and strength, performed by individuals or by synchronized teams. These Finnish women were a gymnastic team in the late 1940s.*

10-25 *The Ukrainian National Relay champions of 1936 were sponsored by the Fort William YMCA. From left to right, they were: P. Tracz, W. Zeleny, A. Slivinski (president), J.J. Stefiszyn, and W. Kozak.*

10-26 *A community-hall dance in Espanola, around 1950. Dances were (and are) an important social event for most communities, giving the residents a chance to mingle and "kick up their heels."*

10-23

10-24

10-25

10-26

claimed their innovation could be used for any event held in an arena, including boxing and wrestling, two other prominent sports in Northern Ontario during the 1930s.

World War II turned attention from sports, as many players enlisted and left the region. When peace came in 1945 and people turned back to peacetime interests, several changes became obvious. The unionization that the war had helped to advance was hostile to the special deals on which industry-supported baseball and hockey teams depended. For a time, at least as far as hockey was concerned, NHL teams supported teams in smaller centres, encouraging players in the farm systems to play for their home team. As the influence of major-league hockey grew and players moved to the larger cities, the smaller centres of Northern Ontario sank into the "B" category. Where games had once been "standing room only," tickets were now given away to attract fans. Television also played its part in this decline; in some arenas television sets were installed to allow fans to watch their favourite shows while attending the local hockey game.

A happy aspect of this shift was the fact that people who might once have relied on competitive sports for entertainment as spectators were becoming active participants, although in other sports. Young people began to enjoy recreational sport much more than competitive sports. Roads built to open up areas for logging operations also opened up new recreational areas, and their virgin lakes and streams attracted hundreds of new sports fishermen, reducing attendance at sports events, especially in the summer. Golf and water sports, not to mention camping, also became popular in the summer, while curling and skiing became more popular in the winter. In these ways, as the "Participaction" campaigns would later emphasize, the shift to recreational sport produced a healthier life for the people of Northern Ontario.

Curling received a boost in 1946, when the Northern Ontario Curling Association was reorganized to allow all Northern Ontario curlers a chance to compete in the National Brier. Only four years later, Tom Ramsay and his Kirkland Lake rink won the 1950 Brier in Vancouver. Northern Ontario did not produce a real contender again until 1971, when the Don Duguid rink finished the round-robin tournament tied with Bill Tetley's rink from Thunder Bay. Tetley lost the playoff, but came back in 1975 to win the Brier and went on to the world championship, where his rink lost the final game by a single stone. Northern Ontario came close in 1979 and 1981 as two more Thunder Bay rinks, the first skipped by Larry Pineau and the second by Al Hackner, finished the Canadian championship in second place. Al Hackner, "The Iceman," came back the following year to sweep all his opponents aside and went on to win the world title in Germany.

This victory matched other sports achievements in Northern Ontario during recent years. Dedication to a sport has to be matched by good facilities and proper training, if successful athletes are to appear. The development of such sports as track and field and swimming was long hampered by a lack of facilities. The growth of Lakehead and Laurentian universities in the 1960s did much to change this situation. The Lakehead Board of Governors had insisted on including an Olympic-size swimming pool in their fine gymnasium, and the university sought the best coaches they could get to train students. The appointment of a world-famous Australian swimming coach, Don Talbot, had dramatic results. By 1975, Joann Baker, a fifteen-year-old member of the Thunder Bay Thunderbolts Swim Club coached by Talbot, had set a Commonwealth record in the 200-metre breaststroke, qualified for the Canadian Can Am and Commonwealth swim teams, and been selected a member of the Canadian swim team for the 1976 Montreal Olympics. The most astonishing achievement was Bill Sawchuk's; after less than five years of Thunderbolt training, he was rated the world's "No. 2" swimmer in the 200-metre individual medley. His performance at the 1978 Commonwealth Games in Edmonton established a new Commonwealth record when he won seven medals: two gold, three silver, and two bronze. This achievement ranked him among the top eight swimmers in the world.

10-27 *A summer camp sponsored by International Co-op Stores Ltd. near Thunder Bay in 1953. Many companies and unions sponsored camps where children could learn outdoor skills.*

Skiing proved to be another area of Lakehead achievement in recent years. A new era began in 1959 with the opening at Mount Baldy by the Port Arthur Ski Club of a 2,400-foot slope served by the only double-chair ski lift between the Canadian Rockies and the Laurentians of Quebec. In 1975, the Big Thunder ski jump was opened to provide one of the best and safest 90-metre jumping hills anywhere in the world. Since then, Big Thunder has been an annual stop for a World Cup weekend. One Thunder Bay native, Steve Collins, became a world contender in 1980 when he flew a record 124 metres at Lahti, Finland, and established himself as the world's best in Nordic competition for juniors from sixteen countries.

Such achievements, to which Alex Baumann's as a member of the Laurentian University Swim Club should be added, demonstrate the importance of fine facilities to sports as a means of recreation. Wintario grants enabled even small communities to build recreation halls with all the modern conveniences. Recreation centres complete with curling clubs and skating rinks, and sometimes swimming pools as well, gave new vigour to sports in many communities. The provincial government has also done a great deal to develop recreational facilities that enable people to enjoy the natural beauties of Northern Ontario. The effort to draw visitors into the region at Minaki and Ogoki lodges may not be commercially successful, but it demonstrates the importance of a recreational potential that Northern Ontarians are able to enjoy whenever they wish. For them, there is no better place to enjoy the good life.

10-27

10-28 *By 1967, when this picture was taken at Five Mile Lake Provincial Park in the Chapleau District, there were scores of provincial parks in the north. Fishing and boating have become recreational activities for the whole family.*

10-29 *The genteel art of fly fishing has declined in popularity with the improvement of the spin-cast rod and reel. Lyle Froyn and June Neilson worked this stream near Sault Ste. Marie in 1948.*

10-30 *The waters of Northern Ontario provide some of the best sailing and cruising waters in the world. Here Miss Demeanor III plies the Lake of the Woods.*

10-28

10-29

10-30

10-31 *Northern Ontario has nurtured world-class downhill and cross-country ski champions who have competed for the World Cup and in the Olympic Games. It all begins at the training stage, where young skiers learn skills and acquire a competitive spirit.*

10-32 *The Thunder Bay area is fortunate in having a number of excellent ski hills. The Loch Lomond ski area is well-known for its wooded trails and double chairlifts.*

10-33 *A popular game everywhere, piggyback races require no special equipment—only strength and skill. These men are competing at the 1981 Lansdowne House Summer Games.*

10-34 *Northern Ontario's rocky wilderness has often been cursed, but the fact remains that wildness is one of the region's major assets. Tourists and residents alike can sightsee on foot, by car, or by rail. Here, hikers admire the Aguasabon Gorge.*

10-31

10-32

10-33

10-34

THE PLACE AND THE PEOPLE

Nelles, H.V. *The Politics of Development: Forests, Mines and Hydroelectric Development in Ontario, 1849-1941*. Toronto: Macmillan, 1974.

Schull, J. *Ontario*. Toronto: McClelland and Stewart, 1972.

Williamson, T.G. *The Northland Ontario*. Toronto: Ryerson Press, 1946.

Wright, J.V. *Ontario Prehistory*. Ottawa: National Museum of Man, 1972.

Zaslow, M. *The Opening of the Canadian North, 1870-1914*. Toronto: McClelland and Stewart, 1971.

EXPLORATION AND THE FUR TRADE

Bishop, Charles A. *The Northern Ojibway and the Fur Trade: An Historical and Ecological Study*. Toronto: Holt, Rinehart and Winston, 1974.

Campbell, Marjorie Wilkins. *The North West Company*. Toronto: Macmillan, 1957.

Campbell, Susan. *Fort William: Living and Working at the Post*. Toronto: Ministry of Culture and Recreation, 1976.

Danziger, Edmund Jefferson. *The Chippewas of Lake Superior*. Norman: University of Oklahoma Press, 1978.

Heidenrich, Conrad E., and Arthur J. Roy. *The Early Fur Trades: A Study in Cultural Interaction*. Toronto: McClelland and Stewart, 1976.

Nute, Grace Lee. *The Voyageur's Highway*. St. Paul: Minnesota Historical Society, 1976.

Rich, E.E. *The Fur Trade and the Northwest to 1857*. Toronto: McClelland and Stewart, 1976.

Williams, Glyndwr. "The Hudson's Bay Company and the Fur Trade: 1670-1870." *The Beaver* 314(2) (Autumn 1983) Special Issue.

TRANSPORTATION AND COMMUNICATIONS

Baum, Arthur W. "The World's Busiest Waterway: The Canal System of the Soo." *Saturday Evening Post* 227(49) (June 4, 1955).

"Fiftieth Year Since Completion of the Ontario Northland Railway 1931-1981: A Commemorative Issue." Graeme Mount and Angus Gilbert, eds. *Laurentian University Review/Revue de l'Universite Laurentienne* 13(2) (February 1981).

Grant, Rev. George M. *Ocean to Ocean: Sandford Fleming's Expedition Through Canada in 1872*. In *Master-Works of Canadian Authors*, vol. 13, ed. John W. Garvin. Toronto: The Radisson Society of Canada, 1925.

Herbert, C.H. "The Development of Transportation in the Canadian North." *Canadian Geographical Journal* 53 (November 1957): 188-98.

McCannel, James. "Shipping on Lake Superior." *Thunder Bay Historical Society Papers* 18 and 19 (1926/1927, 1927/1928): 11-20.

Molson, K.M. *Pioneering in Canadian Air Transport*. Winnipeg: James Richardson & Sons Ltd., 1974.

Nock, O.S. *Algoma Central Railway*. London: Adam & Charles Black, 1975.

Ontario. Department of Lands and Forests. *Early Days: A Record of the Early Days of the Provincial Air Service of Ontario*. Toronto: The Department, 1961.

Stevens, G.R. *Canadian National Railway*. 2 vols. Toronto and Vancouver: Clarke Irwin & Co., 1960-62. Especially vol. 2, *Towards the Inevitable 1896-1922*.

Tucker, Albert. *Steam into Wilderness: Ontario Northland Railway 1902-1962*. Toronto: Fitzhenry and Whiteside, 1978.

West, Bruce. *The Firebirds*. Toronto: Ontario Ministry of Natural Resources, 1974.

LUMBERING, PULP AND PAPER, AND FORESTRY

Hodgins, Bruce W., Jamie Benidickson, and Peter Gillis. "The Ontario and Quebec Experiments with Forest Reserves, 1883-1930." *Journal of Forest History* 26(1) (January 1982): 20-33.

Lambert, Richard S., with Paul Pross. *Renewing Nature's Wealth: A Centennial History of the Public Management of Lands, Forests and Wildlife in Ontario, 1763-1967*. Toronto: Ontario Department of Lands and Forest, 1967.

Lower, A.R.M. *The North American Assault on the Canadian Forest*. Reprint of 1938 ed. New York: Greenwood Press, 1968.

MacKay, Donald. *The Lumberjacks*. Toronto: McGraw-Hill Ryerson, 1978.

Radforth, Ian. "Woodworkers and the Mechanization of the Pulpwood Logging Industry in Northern Ontario, 1950-1970." *Canadian Historical Association Historical Papers* (1982): 71-102.

Swift, Jamie. *Cut and Run: The Assault on Canada's Forests*. Toronto: Between the Lines, 1983.

MINING

Brown, L. Carson. "Ontario's Mineral Heritage." *Canadian Geographical Journal* (March 1968).

Hoffman, Arnold. *Free Gold: The Story of Canadian Mining*. New York: Associated Book Services, 1958.

Lebourdais, D.M. *Metals and Men: The Story of Canadian Mining*. Toronto: McClelland and Stewart, 1957.

MacDougall, J.B. *Two Thousand Miles of Gold: From Val d'Or to Yellowknife*. Toronto: McClelland and Stewart, 1946.

AGRICULTURE AND SETTLEMENT

Arthur, Elizabeth, ed. *Thunder Bay District, 1821-1892: A Collection of Documents*. Toronto: The Champlain Society, 1973.

Barr, Elinor, and Betty Dyck. *Ignace: A Saga of the Shield.* Winnipeg: Prairie Publishing, 1979.

Gourd, Benoit-Beaudry. "La colonisation des Clay Belts du Nord-Ouest québecois et du Nord-Est ontarien." *Revue d'histoire de l'Amerique francaise* 27(2) (Septembre 1973): 235-56.

Hills, G.A. "An Approach to Land Settlement Problems in Northern Ontario." *Canadian Journal of Agricultural Science* 23(4) (December 1942): 212-16.

Newton, Frank H. "The Northern Ontario Clay Belt." *Canadian Magazine of Politics, Science, Art and Literature* 35 (1910): 529-35.

Rumney, George. "Settlement on the Canadian Shield: The Lake Nipissing Area." *Canadian Geographical Journal* 43 (September 1951): 116-27.

Smith, R.M. "Northern Ontario: Limits of Land Settlement for the Good Citizen." *Canadian Geographical Journal* 23 (October 1941): 183-211.

INDUSTRY

Bothwell, Robert, and William Kilbourn. *C.D. Howe, A Biography.* Toronto: McClelland and Stewart, 1979.

MacDowell, Laura Sefton. *Remember Kirkland Lake: The Gold Miners' Strike of 1941-42.* Toronto: University of Toronto Press, 1983.

Morrison, Jean. "Ethnicity and Violence: The Lakehead Freight Handlers Before World War I." In *Essays in Canadian Working Class History*, edited by Gregory S. Kealey and Peter Warrian, 143-160. Toronto: McClelland and Stewart, 1976.

"Northwestern Ontario and After the War." *Labour Review* 4 (1940) 256-60.

Pease, O.C. "In Ontario's Industrial Northland: A Survey of Conditions at the Present Time in the Territory Between Fort William and North Bay." *Industrial Canada* 23(4) (1922): 55-56.

Rasky, Frank. *Industry in the Wilderness.* Toronto and Charlottetown: Dundurn Press, 1983.

Stirrett, J.T. "Factories in Northeast Ontario." *Industrial Canada* 12 (1912) 918-20.

Van Every, Margaret. "Francis Hector Clergue and the Rise of Sault Ste. Marie as an Industrial Centre." *Ontario History* 56 (1964): 191-202.

CITIES AND TOWNS

Collins, Aileen. *Our Town: Sault Ste. Marie Canada.* Vol. 1. Sault Ste. Marie: n.p., 1963.

Kennedy, W.K.P. *North Bay.* North Bay: n.p., 1961.

Hall, Oswald. "The New Planned Community." *Canadian Welfare* 36(1) (January 1960): 9-14.

Mauro, Joseph M. *A History of Thunder Bay.* Thunder Bay: The City, 1981.

Souvenir Booklet Celebrating the Golden Anniversary of the Porcupine Gold Rush. Timmins: Porcupine Golden Anniversary Committee, 1959.

To Our City: A Notre Ville. Sudbury: Sudbury Centennial Committee, 1983.

CULTURE AND THE ARTS

Hodgins, J. George. *Schools and Colleges of Ontario, 1792-1910.* 2 vols. Toronto: L.K. Cameron, 1910.

Lemieux, Germain. *Folklore franco-ontarien.* Sudbury: La Société Historique du Nouvel-Ontario, 1950.

MacDougall, J.B. *Building the North.* Toronto: McClelland and Stewart, 1919.

McLeod, Gordon D. *Essentially Canadian: The Life and Fiction of Alan Sullivan, 1868-1947.* Waterloo: Wilfrid Laurier University Press, 1982.

Morrisseau, Norval. *The Art of Norval Morrisseau.* Lister Sinclair and Jack Pollock, eds. Toronto: Methuen, 1979.

Ritchie, T. *Canada Builds 1867-1967.* Toronto: University of Toronto Press, 1967.

Santana, Hubert de. *Danby: Images of Sport.* Toronto: Amberley House, 1978.

SPORTS AND RECREATION

Babion, Ross. "The Northwestern Ontario Sports Hall of Fame." *Thunder Bay Historical Museum Society Papers and Records* 8 (1980): 1.

Greaves, Joe. "Aspects of Early Sport in Thunder Bay." *Thunder Bay Historical Museum Society Papers and Records* 8 (1980): 2-7.

Littlejohn, Bruce M. "Quetico Country: Wilderness High to Wilderness Recreation." *Canadian Geographical Journal* 71 (1965): 40-55, 78-91.

Pagnucco, Frank. *Homegrown Heroes: A Sports History of Sudbury.* Sudbury: Miller Publishing, 1982.

Priddle, Gerald B. "Parks and Land Use in Northern Ontario." *Environments* 14(1) (1982): 47-51.

ACKNOWLEDGEMENTS

The editors and publishers gratefully acknowledge the assistance of the following individuals in the preparation of this book: Katrin Cooper, Archives of Ontario, Toronto; Pam Hancock, Ontario Ministry of Natural Resources, Toronto; Ken Doherty, Timmins Museum, Timmins; Mary Roche, Sudbury; and Shirley Smith, Winnipeg.

Photo Credits

Algoma Steel Corporation Limited: *1-44, 7-7, 7-12, 7-23, 7-36*
  Ore Division: 5-13, 7-8, 7-9
Anglican Church of Canada — General Synod Archives: *2-1*
Archives des Jesuites de Cormontreuil, France: *4, 5, 6*
Archives des Jesuites, Université de Sudbury. Collège du Sacré-Coeur Collection: *1-24, 9-22*
Archives of the Diocese of Sault Ste. Marie: *1-32*
Archives of Ontario: *1-1, 1-2, 1-3, 1-12, 1-20, 1-26, 1-29, 1-35, 1-36, 1-39, 1-47, 2-3, 2-8, 2-10, 2-11, 2-12, 2-20, 2-21, 2-25, 2-27, 2-37, 2-38, 3-1, 3-5, 3-12, 3-17, 3-18, 3-19, 3-23, 3-24, 3-27, 4-9, 4-20, 4-29, 5-2, 5-5, 5-7, 5-8, 5-11, 5-17, 5-20, 5-24, 5-25, 5-27, 5-37, 6-2, 6-4, 6-6, 6-7, 6-8, 6-10, 6-19, 6-28, 7-6, 7-11, 7-15, 7-16, 7-20, 8-1, 8-5, 8-6, 8-8, 8-9, 8-10, 8-13, 8-19, 8-30, 9-1, 9-15, 9-18, 9-25, 9-31, 10-7, 10-13, 10-24, 10-27*
Arnold, Christina: *15*
Atikokan Centennial Museum: *4-7, 4-18, 4-19, 5-34, 5-36, 9-33, 10-22*
Benson, Crandall and Evadne: *1-14, 2-22, 2-36, 3-9, 3-21*
Black River-Matheson Museum: *4-5, 4-6, 6-11*
Bruce Mines Museum: *8-25*
Canadian Baptist Archives: *1-27, 6-1, 9-3, 9-13*
Canadian Red Cross Society: *8-32*
Caswell, Mr. and Mrs. Ross: *10-3*
Le Centre des Jeunes de Sudbury, Inc.: *9-24*
City of Sault Ste. Marie. Armstrong Collection: *2, 3, 7*
CKSO/CIGM-FM, Sudbury: *3-39*
Cobalt's Northern Ontario Mining Museum: *1-43, 5-15, 5-18*
College of Agricultural Technology, New Liskeard: *6-22, 6-23*
Crawford, Bert: *10-5*
Crawford, Georgina: *21*
Dorion Public Library: *9-9*
Dryburgh, Allan: *6-12, 9-5*
Dryden Observer: *10-16*
Ear Falls District Museum: *3-35*
E.B. Eddy Forest Products Limited: *4-22, 7-33*
Espanola Public Library: *10-26*
Everett, E.C.: *10-6*
Falconbridge Limited, Sudbury Operations. Photo by Dionne Photography: *5-35*
"Fenêtre sur une paroisse: 75e St-David, Noëlville 1905-1980," par C. Mayer, N. Potvin, A. Pitre
  Permission of Hélène Bouffard: 6-20
  Permission of Gilles Daoust: 6-24
Fort Frances Museum and Cultural Centre: *1-7, 1-15, 1-16, 4-17, 4-21, 6-3, 6-14, 8-20, 8-22, 9-23*
Gallagher, Tim: *1-38, 6-26*
Geological Survey of Canada: *7-5 (14278)*
Geraldton Public Library: *5-30, 8-27*
Geraldton-Longlac Times Star: *5-31*
Ginger Ball Collection: *3-6*

Gore Bay Museum (Manitoulin Historical Society Museum, Western Chapter): *3-4, 3-13*
Graver, Cyril: *1-30*
Great Lakes Forest Products Limited: *7-31*
Heritage Centre, Diocese of Algoma: *14, 20, 1-5, 4-16, 7-2*
Howarth, A.C.: *3-7, 6-18, 9-11, 9-16*
Hymers Museum: *1-4, 2-31*
Inco Limited, Ontario Division: *1-40, 5-1, 5-12, 5-19, 5-38*
  Photo by Dionne Photography: 7-37, 7-38
John R. Rigley Collection. Permission of Lori Bouley: *16, 17, 19, 1-25*
Kamstra, Freda: *6-17, 7-29*
Keewatin Public Library: *7-13, 8-31*
Kimberly-Clark of Canada: *3-34*
Lake of the Woods Historical Society: *10-20*
Lake of the Woods Museum: *2-24, 8-15, 10-21*
Lakehead Harbour Commission: *7-19, 7-35*
Lakehead University Library Archives: *5-10, 8-2, 9-6*
Laurentian University Library
  Canadian Mining Journal Collection: 5-22
  Regional Collection: 5-28
  Vincent Crichton Collection: 1-31, 3-8, 3-16
Little Current-Howland Centennial Museum: *11, 1-13, 8-18, 9-17, 10-1*
Marathon Centennial Public Library: *8-24*
Metropolitan Toronto Library. J. Ross Robertson Collection: *2-17*
Minnitaki Tweedsmuir History: *6-13*
Museum of Northern History: *5-6*
New Liskeard and District Museum. Permission of L. Tucker: *5-14, 6-5*
New Liskeard Public Library: *3-31, 3-33, 9-28, 10-9, 10-23*
Nipigon Historical Museum: *1-28, 2-23, 3-14, 4-26, 7-17, 7-18, 10-8*
North Bay and Area Museum: *4-2, 4-10, 9-4, 10-12*
North Bay Nugget: *2-7, 6-27, 8-26*
North Bay Public Library: *1-18, 2-14*
Northwestern Ontario Sports Hall of Fame: *10-2, 10-19, 10-25*
Ojibwe Cultural Foundation: *9-32*
O'Neil, Carolyn: *1-8, 9-12, 10-11*
Ontario Ministry of Education: *9-20, 9-21, 9-29*
Ontario Ministry of Health: *8-33*
Ontario Ministry of Natural Resources
  Chapleau: 18, 2-26, 4-33
  Killarney Provincial Park. Permission of Edgar Loosemore: 6-15
  Toronto: 1-11, 1-22, 1-41, 1-42, 1-46, 2-28, 2-29, 2-30, 2-32, 2-33, 2-34, 2-35, 3-25, 3-28, 3-29, 3-30, 3-38, 4-4, 4-23, 4-24, 4-25, 4-27, 4-28, 4-30, 4-31, 4-34, 4-35, 4-36, 7-21, 7-22, 7-24, 7-25, 7-26, 7-27, 7-30, 7-32, 7-34, 9-7, 9-14, 9-35, 10-17, 10-28, 10-29
  Wawa: 22, 4-11
Ontario Ministry of Northern Affairs: *23*
Ontario Ministry of Tourism and Recreation: *3-15, 9-8, 10-30, 10-31, 10-32, 10-34*
Parent, Sister Huguette, s.c.o.: *1-23, 6-21*
Petterson, Grace: *9-10*
Pukaskwa National Park: *3-36*
Public Archives of Canada: *1-17 (C-26991), 2-2 (C-2771)*
  National Map Collection: 1-9 (24535), 1-10 (8512), 2-9 (13295)
Quetico Provincial Park Archives: *1-6, 1-45*
Rainy River District Women's Institute Museum: *1-21, 1-34, 3-32, 10-14*
Rainy River Public Library: *3-22*
Red Lake Museum: *5-29, 6-16*

Red Rock Public Library: *1-37*

Richards, Ethel: *6-29, 8-17*

Regional Municipality of Sudbury. Photo by Dionne Photography: *8-34,*
    8-35, 8-36

St. Luke's Cathedral, Sault Ste. Marie: *10, 2-13*

Sault Ste. Marie Public Library: *2-6, 3-3, 5-3, 5-16, 6-9, 7-3, 8-3, 8-4, 9-2*

Sioux Lookout Museum: *3-26, 5-23, 10-4*

Spooner, Jessie: *9-19*

Sudbury Public Library
    Mike Solski Collection: 5-33
    North Central Regional Library Collection: 3-10
    Wainwright Collection: 4-8

Sudbury Women's Centre. Miners' Mothers' Day Collection.
    Permission of Norma Kauppi: *3-37*

Temiskaming Speaker: *3-40*

Thunder Bay Historical Museum Society: *1, 8, 9, 12, 13, 2-15, 2-16, 2-18,*
    2-19, 3-2, 3-11, 3-20, 4-15, 6-25, 7-1, 7-4, 7-10, 8-21

Thunder Bay Multicultural Association: *9-26*

Thunder Bay Public Library. Brodie Reference Department: *4-32, 8-23*

Timber Village Museum: *4-3, 4-14*
    Permission of Pat Briere, Sr.: 4-1, 4-12, 4-13
    Permission of T. Quinn: 2-5

Timmins Museum: *1-19, 1-33, 5-4, 5-9, 5-21, 5-26, 5-32, 6-30, 8-11, 8-12, 8-*
    14, 8-28, 8-29, 10-15

Toronto Star. Photo by Dick Loek: *9-30*

Torseth, Mavis (Hewitt): *9-27*

Town of Sturgeon Falls: *2-4, 7-14, 8-16, 9-34, 10-10*

Wawatay News: *7-28, 10-18, 10-33*

Wilson, Mrs. Ira: *8-7*

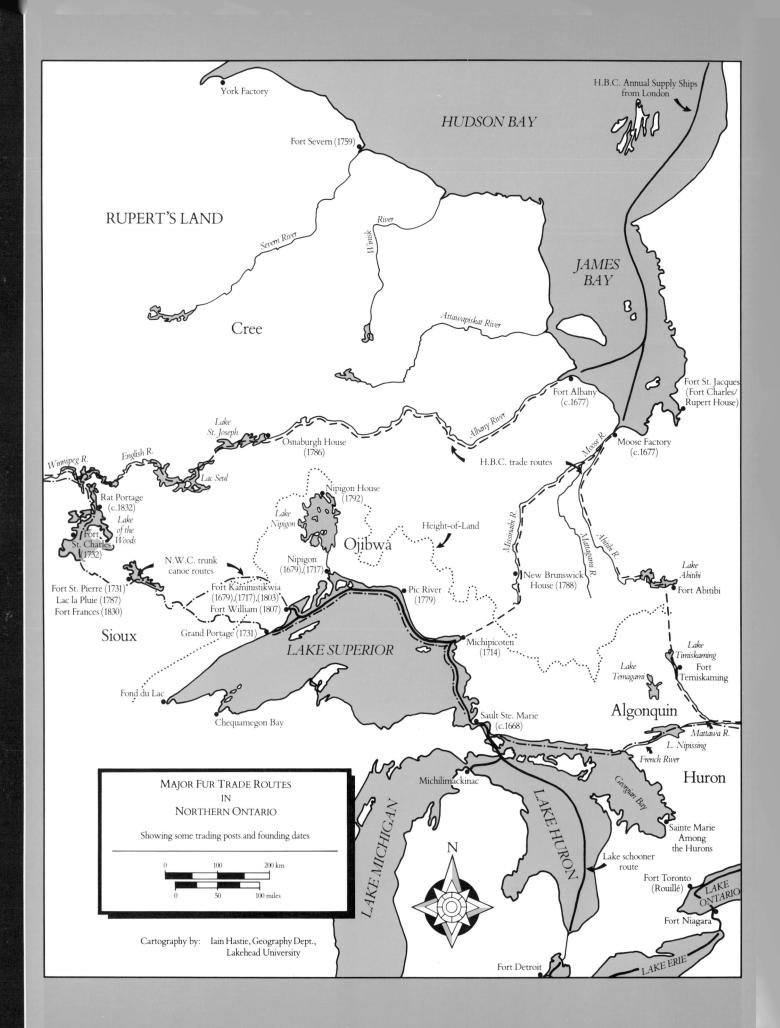

York Factory

HUDSON BAY

Fort Severn (1759)

RUPERT'S LAND

JAMES BAY

H.B.C. Annual Supply Ships
from London

Severn River

Winisk River

Cree

Attawapiskat River

Fort Albany
(c.1677)

Albany River

Fort St. Jacques
(Fort Charles/
Rupert House)

*Lake
St. Joseph*

Osnaburgh House
(1786)

Lac Seul

H.B.C. trade routes

Moose R.

Moose Factory
(c.1677)

Winnipeg R.

English R.

Nipigon House
(1792)

*Lake
Nipigon*

Height-of-Land

Missinaibi R.

Mattagami R.

Abitibi R.

Rat Portage
(c.1832)

*Lake
of the
Woods*

Ojibwa

Nipigon
(1679),(1717)

Fort
St. Charles
(1732)

N.W.C. trunk
canoe routes

Fort Kaministikwia
(1679),(1717),(1803)
Fort William (1807)

Pic River
(1779)

New Brunswick
House (1788)

*Lake
Abitibi*

Fort Abitibi

Fort St. Pierre (1731)
Lac la Pluie (1787)
Fort Frances (1830)

Grand Portage (1731)

LAKE SUPERIOR

Michipicoten
(1714)

*Lake
Temagami*

*Lake
Timiskaming*

Fort
Temiskaming

Sioux

Fond du Lac

Chequamegon Bay

Sault Ste. Marie
(c.1668)

Algonquin

Mattawa R.

L. Nipissing

French River

Huron

Michilimackinac

LAKE MICHIGAN

LAKE HURON

Georgian Bay

Lake schooner
route

Sainte Marie
Among
the Hurons

N

Fort Toronto
(Rouillé)

*LAKE
ONTARIO*

Fort Niagara

Fort Detroit

LAKE ERIE

MAJOR FUR TRADE ROUTES
IN
NORTHERN ONTARIO

Showing some trading posts and founding dates

0   100   200 km

0   50   100 miles

Cartography by: Iain Hastie, Geography Dept.,
Lakehead University

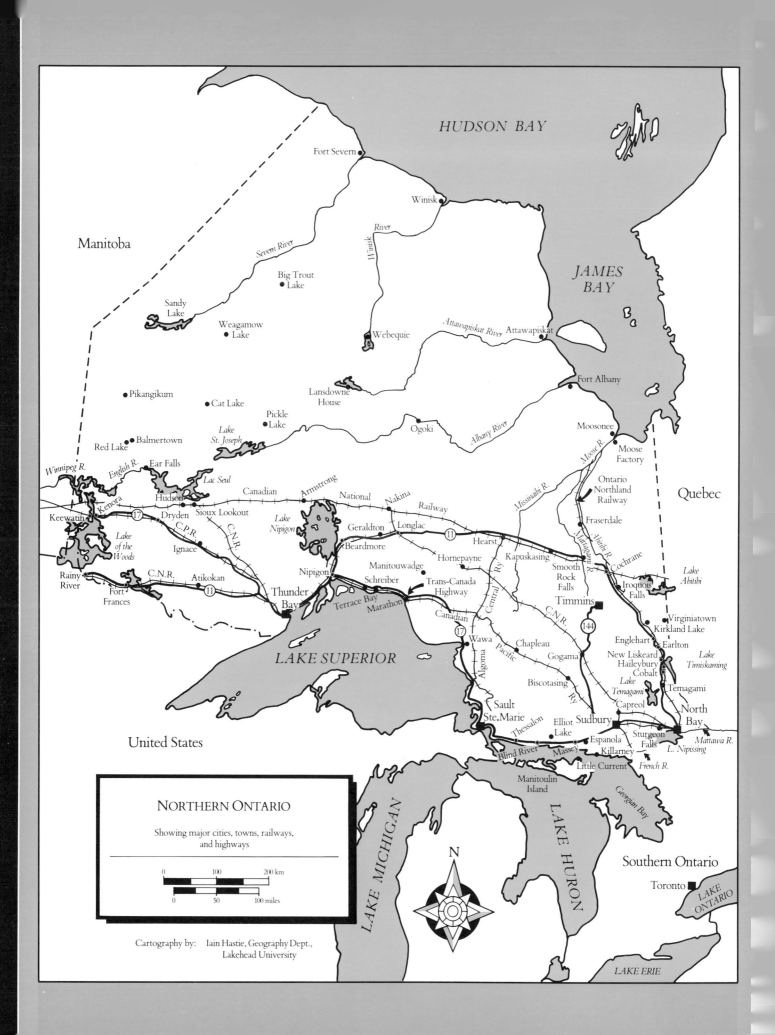

HUDSON BAY

Manitoba

Fort Severn

Winisk

Severn River

Winisk River

River

Big Trout
Lake

JAMES
BAY

Sandy
Lake

Weagamow
Lake

Webequie

Attawapiskat River Attawapiskat

Pikangikum

Cat Lake

Pickle
Lake

Lansdowne
House

Fort Albany

*Lake
St. Joseph*

Ogoki

Albany River

Moosonee

Red Lake Balmertown

Winnipeg R.

English R. Ear Falls

Canadian

Armstrong

National Nakina

Railway

Moose R.

Moose
Factory

Ontario
Northland
Railway

Quebec

Keewatin

Kenora

17

Hudson

Dryden

Sioux Lookout

*Lake
Nipigon*

Geraldton Longlac

11

Hearst

Missinaibi R.

Fraserdale

Abitibi R.

Cochrane

*Lake
Abitibi*

Lac Seul

C.P.R.

Ignace

C.N.R.

Beardmore

Kapuskasing

Mattagami R.

Smooth
Rock
Falls

Iroquois
Falls

Rainy
River

C.N.R.

Atikokan

Nipigon

Schreiber

Manitouwadge

Hornepayne

Timmins

Virginiatown

Kirkland Lake

*Lake
of the
Woods*

Fort
Frances

11

Thunder
Bay

Terrace Bay
Marathon

Trans-Canada
Highway

Canadian

Central Ry.

C.N.R.

144

Englehart

Earlton

*Lake
Timiskaming*

17

Wawa

Chapleau

Gogama

New Liskeard
Haileybury
Cobalt

LAKE SUPERIOR

Algoma

Pacific

Biscotasing

Ry.

*Lake
Temagami*

Capreol

Temagami

North
Bay

Sault
Ste. Marie

Thessalon

Elliot
Lake

Sudbury

Espanola

Sturgeon
Falls

Mattawa R.

L. Nipissing

United States

Blind River

Massey

Killarney

French R.

Little Current

Manitoulin
Island

LAKE
HURON

Georgian Bay

NORTHERN ONTARIO

Showing major cities, towns, railways,
and highways

0   100   200 km

0   50   100 miles

LAKE MICHIGAN

N

Southern Ontario

Toronto

LAKE
ONTARIO

Cartography by: Iain Hastie, Geography Dept.,
Lakehead University

LAKE ERIE